Helping Churches Grow

HELPING CHURCHES GROW

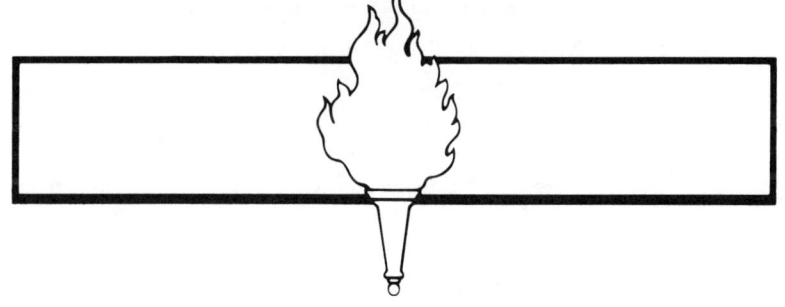

Ralph M. Smith
Bob Edd Shotwell

BROADMAN PRESS
Nashville, Tennessee

GOLDEN GATE SEMINARY LIBRARY

© Copyright 1986 • Broadman Press
All rights reserved
4232-39
ISBN: 0-8054-3239-6
Dewey Decimal Classification: 268
Subject Heading: SUNDAY SCHOOLS // CHURCH GROWTH
Library of Congress Catalog Card Number: 86-4246
Printed in the United States of America

Unless otherwise indicated, Scripture quotations are from the King James Version of the Bible.

Scripture quotations marked (RSV) are from the Revised Standard Version of the Bible, copyrighted 1946, 1952, © 1971, 1973.

Scripture quotations marked (TLB) are from *The Living Bible.* Copyright © Tyndale House Publishers, Wheaton, Illinois, 1971. Used by permission.

Library of Congress Cataloging-in-Publication Data

Smith, Ralph M., 1931-
  Helping churches grow.

  (Broadman leadership series)
  1. Church growth—Southern Baptist Convention.
2. Sunday-schools—Growth.   3. Southern Baptist Convention—Education.   4. Baptists—Education.
I. Shotwell, Bob Edd, 1932-   .   III. Series.
BX6462.7.S45   1986   254'.5   86-4246
ISBN 0-8054-3239-6 (pbk.)

Foreword

It is a special privilege to recommend to you *Helping Churches Grow*. The authors, Ralph M. Smith and Bob Edd Shotwell, are serving in my home church, Hyde Park Baptist Church in Austin, Texas. I served this church as youth minister and minister of education for seven years. I spent a total of thirty years in this church and feel a special warmth for the people, staff, and ministry of this church. Bob Edd and Ralph are among my dearest friends. I love, respect, and admire them and their ministries. They are called and committed men of God. The fruit of their work speak eloquently of what God has wrought through them. They are practicing the methods in this book.

Helping Churches Grow is a book you will want to read and re-read. You will want to refer to and use it often. Practical help for churches to accomplish their mission through the Sunday School and other church organizations literally leaps from these pages. This book should be used by pastors, staff, and laypersons across our nation. This book should be read, given much thought, and then applied. This book gives you the basics, describes them, and tells you how to apply them. This book will assist the church in accomplishing its mission. I encourage you to read and apply this "on the scene" book.

HARRY PILAND
Director, Sunday School Department
The Sunday School Board of the
Southern Baptist Convention

Contents

1. The Importance of the Sunday School 9
   Ralph M. Smith
   Evangelism Enlistment   Enlightenment   Reaching, Teaching, Winning   *The Reaching Arm of the Church   The Teaching Arm of the Church   The Winning Arm of the Church*   Key Organization Concept   Raikes's Definition of a Sunday School
2. Elements in Church Growth 19
   Ralph M. Smith
   The Blessings of God   Sound and Practical Bible Teaching   *Effective Teaching   Preparation and Presentation*   Gifted Leadership   Compassion   Inner Strength   The Spirit of Success   Esprit de Corps   Witnessing Beyond Your Neighborhood   *Advantages of Distance*
3. Maintaining a Growing Sunday School 36
   Bob Edd Shotwell
   Principle One: Make a Commitment to Grow   *Develop a Mind Set for Growth   Set Goals for Growth   Set Goals for the Future*   Principle Two: Identify and Enroll Prospects   Principle Three: Expand the Organization   *Basic Organization   Divisional Organization   Practical Ways to Begin New Units*   Principle Four: Enlist Workers   *Ideal Structure   Methods of Enlisting Workers   Keeping Workers Productive*   Principle Eight: Promote Outreach
4. Developing Quality Education 57
   Bob Edd Shotwell
   Principle Five: Train Workers   Principle Nine: Teach the Bible to Win the Lost and Develop the Saved   *Promote Christian Fellowship   Evaluate Quality*   Principle Six: Provide Adequate Space and Equipment   *Preschool Department   Children's Department   Youth Department   Adult*

Department   *Plan for New Buildings*   Principle Seven: Conduct Weekly Workers Meetings
5. Varied Ministries Contributing to Growth 70
   Bob Edd Shotwell
   Recreation Programs   Senior Adult Program   Weekly Bible Studies   Child Development Center   The Christian School   Camps and Retreats   Sunday School and Other Program Organizations
6. Challenges that Make a Great Church 75
   Ralph M. Smith
   Centering on the Individual   Placing the Kingdom Above the Institution   Multiplying Classes   Overcoming Declining Attendance   Reaching the Youngest and Oldest   Equipping Others to Minister   Every Problem an Opportunity   *A Problem Teacher* Additional Space   A Church in Decline
7. When the Pastor Is the Only Staff Member 92
   Bob Edd Shotwell
   Concluding Thoughts
   Appendixes 96

1
The Importance of the Sunday School
Ralph M. Smith

The work of God is the most important business in the world. Therefore, the work of God should be the best organized and most effective business in the world. The Sunday School is the church organized and functioning to do the work of God. A dynamic Sunday School is uniquely equipped to teach the Bible.

Though the Bible nowhere uses the term *Sunday School,* the Bible continually emphasizes what the goal of the Sunday School is. I believe God gave us the Sunday School to cope with the secular difficulties of reaching people for Christ in today's world.

The Sunday School is the agency of the church designed to carry out the evangelistic and missionary purpose for which the church was founded. In the final meeting Christ had with His church before He ascended into heaven, the agenda was evangelism and world missions. Jesus said, "Go ye therefore, and teach all nations, baptizing them in the name of the Father, and of the Son, and of the Holy Ghost: Teaching them to observe all things whatsoever I have commanded you: and, lo, I am with you alway, even unto the end of the world" (Matt. 28:19-20). This commission commands Christians to evangelize (teach all nations), to enlist (baptizing them), and to enlighten (teaching them to observe all things). All three of these commands can be carried out through the Sunday School.

There is no organization within a church that can accomplish what the Sunday School can. A well-organized Sunday School can become the arm and hand with which the local church does the work of God in a dynamic way.

Perhaps the best illustration I know of the power of the Sunday

School is found in my own life. I grew up in Hot Springs, Arkansas, and attended Second Baptist Church. Unfortunately, neither of my parents were Christians.

When I was five years of age, a friend took me to Sunday School. He was a year older than I, but we attended the same class. This began the most wonderful adventure of my life.

In this small but growing Sunday School, I was taught the Bible. My teacher encouraged us to thank God for His love and goodness. Consequently, I was taught to pray. I learned to give offerings to God through the Sunday School. I made new friends—who, incidentally, are still my friends—and learned the joy of Christian fellowship. In Sunday School, I received my first opportunity to speak in public.

The greatest thing that ever happened to me occurred in Sunday School. One Sunday we had a guest speaker in our fourth-grade department. He gave an invitation in the departmental assembly. I was on a pew in the back, singing the invitational hymn. Mrs. Roy Bayles, the departmental superintendent, leaned over from the row behind me and asked if I did not want to become a Christian. My response was negative. The Holy Spirit, however, was convicting me of my need to receive Jesus as my Savior. That Sunday afternoon I confirmed in my heart the decision I knew I needed to make. I was saved by God's grace.

Heaven-sent Sunday School teachers had planted the gospel seed in my heart. A dedicated Sunday School superintendent urged me to publicly respond to the evangelist's plea. My conversion was the result of a Sunday School sharing the love of Jesus and His gospel.

In the following years of my life, the Sunday School taught me the Bible week by week. This was the only spiritual instruction I received. In ways that are beyond my knowing, the Holy Spirit through the Sunday School helped me to grow in my knowledge of the Bible and thus helped me to grow spiritually. I was certainly far from what I should have been as a child and teenager, but without the Sunday School's influence, I shudder to think what would have become of me.

I believe in the Sunday School! My testimony is not unique. Tens of thousands can give the testimony I have given. Sunday School teachers, directors, and workers have led multitudes of children, teenagers, and adults to a saving knowledge of Jesus Christ. Seldom does a Sunday pass in our church without someone walking down the aisle to confess Christ as Savior. Often a Sunday School teacher, director, or member accompanies the new convert down the aisle.

Evangelism

The first purpose of the church is to reach every possible person, share the gospel, and witness to Christ. The Great Commission is doubly clear as to territory. Christ tells us to go into all the world. That covers the territorial expanse of the universe. He further commands us to "make disciples of all nations" (Matt. 28:20, RSV), which means every human being. Jesus taught His disciples "The field is the world" (Matt. 13:38). I believe that the Sunday School is the key organization to help churches fulfill the challenges in the Great Commission. Thus, the Sunday School is the key to church growth.

Virtually every church begins small. Most leaders want their churches to grow spiritually and numerically. If a church is to grow, it must reach beyond its immediate neighborhood. Many large churches have declined because of a "neighborhood" mentality. While it is true that the Sunday School should first try to reach its neighborhood, it is false to believe that this is the fulfillment of its task. Jesus said, "Ye shall be witnesses unto me both in Jerusalem, and in all Judaea, and in Samaria, and unto the uttermost part of the earth" (Acts 1:8). Please notice that Jesus did *not* say, "Be witnesses unto me in the northwest corner of Jerusalem," nor did He say, "in your neighborhood in Jerusalem."

The field of our witness is the world, and we must never cease our efforts in witnessing and evangelism until the last unsaved person has been converted, baptized, and discipled. When planning evangelistic outreach, we should consider no distance too far. People will drive or come as far to church as they do to work, to buy groceries, to attend the theater. Recently, a man joined our church who lives fifty miles away.

Enlistment

The second great command in the Great Commission is a vital task of the church. Christ told us to baptize those who are saved. One point where some of our Sunday Schools are failing is in not encouraging new converts to publicly declare their faith in Christ by believer's baptism. Baptism does not save. We are saved by grace through faith in Christ (Eph. 2:8-9). Baptism is not the gospel (1 Cor. 1:17; 15:1-4,11). Baptism is, however, very important.

Christ was baptized by John the Baptist in the Jordan River. Jesus lived in Nazareth. It is approximately forty miles from Nazareth to where John was baptizing in the Jordan River. Jesus walked forty miles to be baptized. Baptism must have been extremely important to our Lord. When Jesus was baptized, He identified Himself with humanity. When we are baptized, we identify ourselves with Deity.

The church and its program organizations should encourage converts to follow Jesus in New Testament baptism. When new converts are baptized, they publicly declare that they believe that Jesus died, was buried, and was resurrected from the grave. It is the converts' outward expression of inner faith. When Jesus was baptized, He identified Himself with us. When we are baptized, we identify ourselves with Him.

When a person is saved and follows Christ in baptism, he or she becomes a member of the local New Testament church. Dr. Luke wrote in Acts: "Then they that gladly received his word were baptized: and the same day there were added unto them about three thousand souls" (Acts 2:41).

Enlightenment

A new Christian must know what to believe and how to behave. Therefore, teaching is a mandatory step in obeying the Great Commission. Jesus commanded us, "[teach] them to observe all things" (Matt. 28:20). The Sunday School should be more effective than any other organization in the church in teaching the Bible. Teaching is always the imperative need in our churches. When we neglect the important function of follow-up teaching, we have not completely carried out the Great Commission.

Francis Bacon said, "Some books are to be tasted, others to be swallowed, and some few to be chewed and digested." The Bible is the Book of books. It is to become a part of life. Christian education does not mean teaching people to know what they do not know; it means teaching them to behave as they do not behave. We will never see a time when we do not need to be taught God's Word. Ignorance is not innocence, but sin!

Those who are saved will drift in their commitment to Christ if they do not have strong Bible teaching to anchor their faith. The tug of the world, their sinful nature, and the temptations of Satan will draw them away from Christ and their best intentions. A Bible teaching Sunday School is a great force in building up Christians in the faith and preserving a strong New Testament church.

There is a tendency in today's churches that will weaken our Christian witness and spell ruin in the churches. Some churches are building on the dynamic personality of their pastor and have little Bible teaching. Others are building on special days, promotions, gimmicks, and contests. There are still other trends among churches where the ministry is based solely on music, emotion, buildings, missionary outreach, recreation, or an action-oriented program to youth. While all these concepts and ministries have a legitimate place, they have neglected the heart of the Great Commission.

Jesus commanded us, "Go ye therefore, and teach . . . Teaching them to observe all things." Teaching is the great need in all of our churches. With each new generation, there is a new challenge to teach the message of the Bible. The church that builds on the Sunday School grows stronger with the passing years because the Sunday School is where teaching the Bible is predominant.

This approach has certainly proved effective at Hyde Park Baptist Church. In 1957, our church built the West Education Building. Quickly, this space was filled, and the Sunday School average attendance increased to 850.

In 1967, the church built a three-story, 45,000-square-foot East Education Building. The average Sunday School attendance grew to over 1,000. The growth made it necessary to renovate the sanctuary and increase the seating.

In 1973, the church built the South Education Building, and average attendance climbed to 1,326. Meanwhile, we established a new mission and sent 150 from our Sunday School to the new mission.

The following year, the church built a beautiful Fellowship Hall and Family Life Center. Both of these spaces were used for Sunday School and average attendance grew to well over 1,400.

In 1978, we completed the East Education Complex with a 30,000 square foot educational building. Sunday School average attendance soared to over 1,800 each Sunday with an enrollment of 4,239. By 1982, enrollment had climbed to 5,359 with an average weekly attendance of 2,240.

As Hyde Park Baptist Church started to build each of the last three buildings, some of our people said, "We need a larger sanctuary." They were correct. During this time, our 1,100-seat sanctuary was filled to capacity at both the 8:30 and 11:00 AM worship hours. In fact, in 1968, we had renovated the sanctuary and enlarged it to seat 300 additional people. For three years, we had three morning worship services, and at 11:00 AM, we used overflow closed-circuit TV in the Fellowship Hall. We even had a special worship service for children in the Family Life Center. Instead of building a new sanctuary, however, we continued to build Sunday School space.

The Importance of the Sunday School

Sunday School is the undergirding church organization. When we talk about the church *organized* to carry out the Great Commission, we are talking about the Sunday School.

Finally, in 1983, we entered our new 2,600-seat sanctuary. Prior to that, we had built a five-story, 510-car parking structure. But even when we built the sanctuary, we added more Sunday School space. At the writing of these lines, our Sunday School is averaging 2,700 or more each Sunday. We have just named a building study committee to plan a great new five-story, 55,000-square-foot educational building, and a new Family Life Center.

Currently, we are planning and building for a Sunday School enrollment of 10,000. At that time, we should have an average Sunday School attendance of around 5,000. By the grace of God and under the leadership of His Holy Spirit, we believe that we will reach these people and more.

I believe your church can grow. Jesus taught, "According to your faith be it unto you" (Matt. 9:29).

The best way to build a strong, dynamic New Testament church is by building strong program organizations, especially a great Sunday School. In the following pages, we will discuss how your church can grow numerically and spiritually through the Sunday School and other organizations. Perhaps the only limitation is vision, for "where there is no vision, the people perish" (Prov. 29:18).

It is possible to grow a mushroom in a very short time. But decades are required to grow a great, sturdy oak tree. Some churches mushroom. They soar like a skyrocket. But I have observed that they fall down as quickly as they spring up. Mushrooms are not very strong or stable. Great churches and Sunday Schools take time, tears, prayers, and hard work to build. But they are worth the effort.

Reaching, Teaching, Winning

The Old Testament verse that has historically been used to describe the ministry of the Sunday School is Deuteronomy 31:12:

"Gather the people together, men, and women, and children, and thy stranger that is within thy gates, that they may hear, and that they may learn, and fear the Lord your God, and observe to do all the words of this law." The three aspects of the Sunday School are outlined in this verse.

The Reaching Arm of the Church

Sunday School is the reaching arm of the church. "Gather the people together, men, and women, and children, and thy stranger that is within thy gates." Sunday School brings together both saved and unsaved for Christian instruction. The verse implies a central point of assembly. The word *ekklesia* (church) in the New Testament comes from *assembly*.

The Teaching Arm of the Church

Sunday School is the teaching arm of the church. The command says: "that they may hear, and that they may learn, . . . and observe to do all the words of this law." Undoubtedly, the Sunday School is to be evangelistic, but the Sunday School is to be more than evangelistic. In Sunday School, the Word of God is taught to all Christians so that they may grow in grace in the knowledge of our Lord and Savior, Jesus Christ. The principle is that we should reach people where they are and, through teaching, lift them to where they should be.

The Winning Arm of the Church

Sunday School is the winning arm of the church. The command goes on to say: "and fear the Lord your God." The Old Testament states that the fear of the Lord is the beginning of wisdom (Prov. 1:7). That phrase is an Old Testament term for salvation. Today we Christians use the terms *believe, trust,* or *receive.* In the Old Testament, the word *fear* was used.

Key Organization Concept

The Sunday School is the key organization in the life of the church. The success of all other organizations in the church is directly related to the growth and success of the Sunday School. The Sunday School is the great Bible teaching agency of the church. It is the organization through which the church receives much of its money. The Sunday School is the organizational heart of the church. Through its classes and departments, the Sunday School becomes the ministering arm of the church. The Sunday School is a way to reach people who would be otherwise unreached. Moreover, Sunday School gives many people an opportunity to work for Christ and to win others to the Lord.

Raikes's Definition of a Sunday School

The church began during the earthly ministry of our Lord (Matt. 16:13-19; 18:15-20). Robert Raikes began the Sunday School, as we know it, in 1780.

First, the Sunday School involves factual instruction of the Bible as the Word of God. In Raikes's day, instruction was predominantly the catechism in religious education.

There are many ways to teach the Bible, such as topically, doctrinally, biographically, or textually. Sunday School teachers, with the help of curriculum materials, should take advantage of many approaches to teaching in order to reach people for Christ and to instruct them regarding the elements of Christian living. Teachers should be careful to emphasize the unity of the Bible and to maintain the interest of class members.

Second, the Sunday School uses laypersons to teach and administer the program. In Raikes's day, the clergy predominantly taught religious education. Laymen were seldom used to teach the Bible. Today most Sunday School teacher are laypersons.

The involvement of laypersons is one of the most vital contributions a Sunday School makes in the life of the church. It develops laypeople into excellent Bible students and teachers. It gives the laity of the church teaching and witnessing responsibility. It makes the whole church program a team effort and not totally dependent on the minister or ministers.

Third, the Sunday School centered on the children of the streets, not just the children of church members. In Raikes's day, many clergymen fought the Sunday School, refusing the ruffians of the street access to the church.

Outreach is a vital concept in a dynamic Sunday School. A church ministering only to its members is failing to carry out Jesus' final teaching before He ascended into heaven. He gave a specific command: "As you are going about in the world, make disciples and teach them to observe the things I have commanded you" (Matt. 28:19-20, author's paraphrase).

Finally, the purpose of the Sunday School was evangelistic: to bring pupils to Christ.

Our modern Sunday Schools might well follow these four principles of Raikes: factual instruction of the Bible; the use of laypersons to teach the Bible; a major focus on outreach and bringing new people to church; the primary purpose of evangelism.

How do Raikes's concepts translate into the modern Sunday School? The Bible is relevant in today's world. There is a stunning ignorance of the Bible. An effective Sunday School will major on teaching the Bible. There is a difference between teaching the Bible and teaching "about" the Bible.

Laypersons make excellent Sunday School teachers. Christianity began as a lay movement. Among the twelve disciples, there was not a single priest or Levite. Those men were able to turn the world upside down.

An effective Sunday School will seek to reach beyond the four walls of the church. Its members will bring their families, friends, associates, and others to Sunday School and worship services. The church that does not preach and practice outreach will perish.

These efforts will culminate in evangelism. The lost will be saved. Joy will be in heaven over the lost coming to know Jesus Christ as personal Savior.

2
Elements in Sunday School Growth
Ralph M. Smith

The Blessings of God

Churches and Sunday Schools grow because God blesses them. This is a New Testament truth. What caused the dynamic growth of the first century church? God blessed these early Christians, and dramatically the church grew.

There were 120 Christians in the upper room praying before Pentecost. On the day of Pentecost, 3,000 were converted. Later, 5,000 united with the church in a single service. It is estimated that just a few months after the ascension of Christ, the church in Jerusalem had grown to 20,000 members. How could this tremendous growth be explained apart from the blessings of God?

I have often been asked to explain the continued growth of our Sunday School at Hyde Park Baptist Church. The following pages will outline how a Sunday School should be organized, proven steps in church growth, the maintenance of the Sunday School, and factors in growth and building easily overlooked. From a human standpoint, I believe our Sunday School has grown because it teaches the Word of God. I try to preach the Word of God, the Bible. Our staff seeks to follow the leadership of the Holy Spirit. We have some of the most dedicated teachers and workers in God's kingdom. Our members love the Lord and one another.

Having said that, I would quickly add that *this is not the ultimate reason I believe our Sunday School grows and progresses.* I firmly believe God has blessed our church, and that is why it prospers. May the great God whom we know through Jesus Christ and the Holy Spirit be praised. He shares His glory with no man. And if we have any glorying to be done, it must be done to God!

God has not blessed our church because I am unique, talented, or dedicated. God has not blessed our church because we have a great staff, though I believe there is no better staff anywhere. Our location is judged by some to be poor. The church is not a young church in the suburbs. It was founded in 1894. We are an inner city church in an old neighborhood. There are many apartments around the church. To me, the members are the greatest, but you might judge them as average and normal.

How, then, do I explain the growth of Hyde Park Baptist Church (last year over seven hundred people joined our church, and the Sunday School enrollment grew by nearly six hundred persons)? I would say God has chosen to bless our church. Praise His name! This does not mean we are not to pray, work, witness, enlist, and train. God blesses the churches which do those things. Our church grows because God chooses to bless the work we do in His name and to His glory. Joyfully I sing:

> Praise God, from whom all blessings flow;
> Praise Him, all creatures here below;
> Praise Him above, ye heav'nly host;
> Praise Father, Son, and Holy Ghost.

Sound and Practical Bible Teaching

The central task of the Sunday School is to teach the Bible. An effective Sunday School will unceasingly and effectively teach God's Word. The Bible is profitable for doctrine, reproof, correction, and instruction in the Word of God (2 Tim. 3:16). It matures the Christian. To the new convert, the Bible is like milk. To the mature Christian, the Bible is like strong meat. Indeed, it is sweet like honey. As the Bible is taught to the Christian disciples, believers grow in grace and in the knowledge of the Lord and Savior, Jesus Christ.

People have been and always will be attracted by the Word of

God. Sunday Schools with leaders who believe, teach, and practice the doctrines of the Bible grow. Conversely, those Sunday Schools without such leaders, where the Bible is not taught, do not grow and usually decline in attendance.

Teaching God's Word is vitally important to Christians. Bible teaching changes attitudes and outlooks. Soul-winners are more effective as they are taught the Bible. Faith is solidified through Bible study. The mind is made alert and observant. Most important of all, believers' prayer life is strengthened as they are taught and study the Bible. Sunday Schools built on solid Bible teaching will grow numerically and deepen the spiritual lives of the pupils who attend. The apostle Peter promised, "The Word of the Lord endureth forever" (1 Pet. 1:25).

Many denominational publishing houses provide excellent helps for Bible study in Sunday School. The Bible, however, is to be the textbook. Sunday School members should be encouraged to bring their Bibles to class. Class members should read from the Bible, not the quarterly. Class members should be encouraged to memorize the Bible. The psalmist wrote, "Thy word have I hid in mine heart, that I might not sin against thee" (Ps. 119:11). A dusty Bible means a dirty heart.

Sunday School teachers should believe in the complete inspiration of the Bible. No one can estimate the damage a heretical teacher can cause. One who is a doubter should keep those doubts to oneself. We are to teach what we believe—not what we disbelieve. Paul instructed the young preacher Timothy: "All scripture is given by inspiration of God, and is profitable for doctrine, for reproof, for correction, for instruction in righteousness: That the man of God may be perfect, throughly furnished unto all good works" (2 Tim. 3:16-17). Any Sunday School teacher who denies the reliability of the Bible should quietly be asked to join a class and let another teach. If a Sunday School teacher must be replaced, it should be done in the kindest and tenderest way possible.

Teaching is a gift (Rom. 12:7). Without this gift of the Spirit, the teacher will have little success. Some who are failing at teaching may be excellent departmental directors. Some who cannot teach adults effectively may be tremendous teachers in preschool classes. Leaders in the Sunday School must be sensitive and discerning to changes that are necessary. An inept teacher will hurt the spiritual life of the teacher and usually weaken the class.

Jesus Christ, our Lord, was often referred to as "Teacher." It is most interesting that the Gospels emphasize teaching as a priority. The Gospel writers place the word *teaching* before *preaching* when referring to the ministry of Christ. "And Jesus went about all the cities and villages, teaching in their synagogues, and preaching the gospel of the kingdom, and healing every sickness and every disease among the people" (Matt. 9:35). Teaching was sowing the seed, and preaching was reaping the harvest.

Effective Teaching

The Sunday School teacher should seek to teach the Bible as effectively as possible. The aim of the teacher is first to get the Bible into the pupil's mind and heart. Second, the teacher should try to get the pupil into personal Bible study. This is called double transference.

The Sunday School teacher should not be content with telling jokes, relating news events of the past week, or talking about church programs. The Sunday School teacher has a mandate to teach the Bible, which is the Word of God. God has promised to bless His Word. He further promises that, when taught, the word will not return unto Him void (Isa. 55:11).

If Sunday School teachers are to be effective, they must know their pupils. Sunday School teachers should remember that they are teaching people and not just lesson content. Contacts outside of the class are most important.

Teaching should be done in such a way that individual needs are met. I believe that the best way to teach is to teach the scriptural content, illustrate the scriptural content, and apply the scriptural content to individual needs. The teacher has not completed the task until the lesson is made relevant and helpful.

Elements in Sunday School Growth

The physical is vitally related to the spiritual. If a classroom is poorly lighted or if there is a noise or distraction taking place, it is difficult to teach. If a pupil is having a personal problem financially or physically, it is difficult to teach that pupil. Emotional needs should also be taken into consideration. If there is any hindrance that the teacher senses, one should seek its removal so that one can better impart the Word of God.

Preparation and Presentation

Teaching a Sunday School class is a serious responsibility. If carpenters or craftsmen should spoil a piece of material they are working upon, they can throw it aside and take another piece; but the teacher cannot do this with a person created in God's image. Francis Bacon was correct when he wrote, "A man is but what he knoweth."

I want to write directly at this point to the Sunday School teachers and future teachers who are reading this book. If teachers prepare and present adequately the lesson, they will take the following things into account:

1. Lesson preparation should begin early in the week, preferably even Sunday afternoon. This will help the teacher relate experiences he has during the week to the lesson the following Sunday.

2. Earnestly pray during the week for the leadership of God's Holy Spirit as you teach the lesson on Sunday. We can do much after we pray, but little or nothing before we pray. There are more than three-hundred prayer promises in the Bible. The wise teacher will claim them.

3. During your prayer time, pray for each pupil in the class. Ask God to help you to meet the needs of the class as a whole and the pupils individually. If your class is large, pray for a given number of your class members daily. Divide the class roll by seven, the days of the week, and pray for one seventh of your class daily.

4. By Wednesday night, develop the main points that you intend to emphasize. Usually the lesson will have a central theme that is stated in the Sunday School quarterly. Seek the help of

other teachers by attending teachers and officers meetings on Wednesday night. Use the church library in developing your points and central theme.

5. Devise an interesting way to capture the class's attention as you first begin to teach the lesson. You may choose to give the background of the lesson, relate a news event, use an anecdote, tell a personal experience or an illustration.

6. One of the best ways to teach the lesson is to give the biblical content. This will take several minutes. Second, illustrate the biblical content so that it is clearly understood as to its meaning and background. Third, apply the biblical content to meet the needs in the individual pupil's lives. All of these features can be achieved as teachers present the material and guide the interaction and discussion within their classes.

7. It is good to leave time at the end of the class to allow pupils to ask questions. You might also have questions during the class period. Do not let the questioning get out of hand so as to consume the entire class period. This is only a part of teaching.

8. Try to learn the lesson material so thoroughly that you are not tied to notes. Above all, teach from the Bible, not from the quarterly or commentary. Remember, telling is not teaching; listening is not learning.

9. Never embarrass class members. For example, do not call on class members to pray unless you know they are happy to lead in prayer. It is best to ask them in private if they will lead the class prayer. Some class members do not read well. If a teacher asks that class member to read a verse of Scripture, the teacher may embarrass that member.

10. The wise teacher will not get sidetracked from the lesson or its application. Class members have personal problems; sometimes they want to verbalize these. If this can be done briefly, it may prove helpful. Generally, however, the teacher should offer to visit with the class member after class and continue with the lesson. Many a Sunday School class period has been dominated by one member with a personal problem. This is discouraging to the class.

Be careful that one member does not consume the class teaching time.

11. Repetition is helpful. Classes enroll new members who need to be taught the "old" truths. Unfortunately, some students do not receive the message the first time it is taught. "Of course, everything has been said that needs to be said—but since no one was listening, it has to be said again," wrote an unknown author.

Someone has defined teaching as guiding the learning experience of the pupils. This kind of teaching would involve at least three characteristics. First, the teacher must *know* the material intellectually and personally. Second, the teacher tries to *relate* the material to experiences in the lives of the pupils that lead to definite Christian living. Third, the teacher is *communicating* with the pupil and not just reciting what is known about the biblical content.

Gifted Leadership

The difference between a growing church and a stagnant one is pastoral leadership. Gifted men build great churches, and average men build average churches. Inspired leadership is a God-given gift (a natural gift as well as a spiritual gift). God's solution has always been to send a man or a woman to lead. When God wanted to lead Israel from Egyptian bondage, He called Moses. When God wanted Israel to take the Promised Land, He called Joshua. When God needed a judge in Israel, He called Deborah. When He wanted a builder for churches in Europe, He sent Paul. Today, when God wants His work done, He calls people to do it.

In some churches, pastoral leadership will mean only the pastor. In other churches, it will refer to more than one person. In the New Testament, there seemed often to be two or more pastors leading one church. When I speak of pastoral leadership at Hyde Park Baptist Church, I am talking about all of our ministers: pastor, minister of education and administration, minister of music, associate pastor, business coordinator, minister to singles and students, minister of youth education, minister of childhood education, recreation director, Chinese pastor, Korean pastor, and Spanish pastor.

If a pastor seeks to maintain control of every ministry in the church and every facet of Sunday School, he will probably lead a small church. The inability of some churches to grow is sometimes the inability of the pastor (or the pastors) to relinquish leadership to others. Remember the church and Sunday School started out as lay movements.

I rejoice when our staff members are loved by the people. It is a sign of their strength and leadership ability when they faithfully discharges their responsibilities. The senior pastor should never feel threatened when other ministers in the church are effective in showing leadership ability. The senior minister should be concerned only when other ministers are not leading effectively and are not being well received by the congregation.

When a pastor is the single staff member of the church, one *must* assume leadership of the Sunday School. The pastor of this congregation should organize the Sunday School, conduct the teachers and officers meetings, train and inspire the workers. A layperson may be the Sunday School director, but the pastor has to be the leader.

The good and godly layperson can only donate limited time to being Sunday School director. The Sunday School should be on the pastor's mind all the time. Many a small Sunday School fails because an untrained layperson Sunday School director is expected by the pastor to be a full-time educational director. Pastor, if you are the only staff member at your church, you have an awesome responsibility, but *you* have it!

When I was called to be pastor of the First Baptist Church in Rosenberg, that marvelous church had a Sunday School attendance of slightly over two hundred. We did not have a minister of education, but we had a dedicated layperson, Mr. Don Bryant, the newspaper editor, who served as our Sunday School superintendent. He did a marvelous job.

I asked Don if he would object if, when we needed teachers and

I knew of someone who could fill the position, I would get a teacher for the Sunday School. I assured him that I would keep him informed so that he and I would not both be enlisting a teacher for the same class. We worked together for four years. During that time, there was never one moment of conflict. I enlisted teacher after teacher, and he enlisted teacher after teacher. We worked together as a team.

I am convinced that, had I left it up to him to enlist all the teachers, our Sunday School would have been hurting. He was the director. The responsibility was his, but I was the pastor and the total responsibility was mine. We worked together! In most of our churches, the pastor is the best-trained person in the church in religious education. He dares not default in his responsibility to lead the Sunday School, the key organization in the church. Of course, the church is greatly blessed that is able to call a godly minister of education to assume leadership in the Sunday School.

Gifted leadership is God-given. Such gifted leadership is one generation long and cannot be passed to followers. The pastor using charisma correctly will help individuals to change their lives and provide leadership to help a dying or lethargic church to grow and succeed.

The pastor with *false humility* can never be the leader of a great and growing congregation because his personality will not allow it. Humility is a golden virtue! False humility can lead to the defeat of a church.

The gifted leader will appeal to absolutes, to tradition, to experts, and to the will of the governed.

The wise pastor will first appeal to the absolutes of the Word of God. The Sunday School is designed to teach the Bible. There can be no higher or better authority. The gifted leader will appeal to the deep feelings of the congregation. Truly gifted leaders believe that they will not and cannot fail.

Some pastors do not grow in their leadership ability because they are unwilling to risk and to extend themselves. Gifted leaders do not simply take the easy and safe route. They live by faith and risk themselves. Just as there is no victory without a fight, there are no successes in the Lord's work without attempting great things for God. A pastor who is afraid of failure will not build a great Sunday School or church.

Compassion

The New Testament says that Jesus looked down upon the city of Jerusalem and wept over it. Paul indicated that he shed tears over the church (Acts 20:19, 31). Jeremiah, the prophet of the Old Testament, said, "My eyes have run rivers of tears" (Jer. 9:1, author's paraphrase). Great churches and Sunday Schools are built out of a spirit of compassion for the unsaved.

The word *compassion* is a compound of two words meaning "to suffer with." This is a heart set on fire with a desire to reach the unchurched and win the lost to Christ. When teachers have compassion, their classes will grow. When department directors love God and the unsaved, they naturally will want to expand their departments and reach out to the unchurched and unsaved.

A pastor, education director, or departmental director should never *use* people to build the church. The people are the church. If the leader loves people and ministers to them, numerical growth will be the result.

Inner Strength

Churches grow because of inner strength. They do not necessarily grow because of organization or techniques. When the root system of a tree is healthy, the tree tends to become taller, spread its branches, and bear fruit. The roots tap the source of growth, and fruit is produced. The same is true of a growing, dynamic, fruit-bearing Sunday School.

The ministry in many evangelical churches is measured by its ability to meet needs. However, needs are not the only basis for establishing the strategy for church ministry. Meeting needs can produce self-centered Christians, resulting in a humanistic program centering on the pupil. If needs are viewed through the eyes of God so that the pupil is seen as a sinner, needing salvation and spiritual growth, then the Sunday School will expand. Strategy is formulated on biblical imperatives from which needs are viewed. The center of ministry should be relevant to the Scriptures and not vice versa.

Organizations do not produce power or growth. Organization is a vehicle through which power is channeled. Methods, programs, and organizations are not causal factors for growing New Testament churches. In point of fact, organization that results in institutionalization might harm growth.

Dr. J. N. Barnett did a marvelous service when he wrote *The Pull of the People* (1956) and listed "The Laws of Sunday School Growth." Some Southern Baptists believe that by following these "laws," Southern Baptists have grown to be the nation's largest evangelical denomination. I do not agree and believe Dr. Barnett would also disagree.

Sunday School growth is a result of a strong evangelistic thrust of churches. The laws of growth were used mightily by God to organize and consolidate the gains from evangelistic outreach. When Southern Baptist churches cease to emphasize evangelistic outreach, they cease to grow.

Critics claim the Sunday School is dying. Some churches have witnessed a decline of their Sunday Schools. However, many Sunday Schools among the evangelicals are experiencing growth.

The Spirit of Success

Some Sunday Schools are filled with such a spirit that we know they are going to grow spiritually and numerically. When we enter the church buildings, we are aware of a contagious enthusiasm. They have a spirit of success. When a church is pulsating with this spirit of success, it attracts new families.

A group of workers in an office were outproducing all other branches of their company. Management wanted to discover their secret of success. On the surface, there was no apparent reason. Management added thirty minutes to their lunch period, and production increased. Management allowed them to go home thirty minutes early, and production went up. Management added fifteen minutes to the morning and afternoon coffee breaks, and production increased, though the workday had now been shortened by two full hours!

Management then reversed the whole process. They took away the coffee breaks, lengthened the work day, and shortened the lunch period. What was the result? Production again increased! The spirit within the office made the difference!

When there is the intangible spirit of success within the Sunday School, good things happen. This is true to Bible doctrine.

Paul and Silas were thrown in jail in Philippi. That did not deter their determination to obey Christ's commission. It only moved the revival from the street to the jail. The prisoners in the jail were converted. The jailor and his family were saved. There was a revival at midnight in Philippi (Acts 16:25-34).

A joyful, thankful, optimistic spirit . . . a spirit of success . . . the Spirit of Christ . . . the Holy Spirit is bound to prevail. Pray to God that you will have this spirit. Do all within your power to instill it in your Sunday School.

Nothing succeeds like success. This is a threadbare saying, but it is true: "Wherever you find the spirit of success, you will find a growing, dynamic Sunday School."

Esprit de Corps

A vital factor in Sunday School growth is esprit de corps. When the Sunday School has a group spirit and a sense of pride and honor in what is being accomplished, a great Sunday School can be built and effective work can be done.

Magnetism develops in a Sunday School where the Holy Spirit fills the director, teachers, and leaders. This group spirit is winsome and contagious. Christianity is caught as well as taught. I believe the spirit of success is a dynamic factor in building esprit de corps in a Sunday School. People will respond to a great challenge.

Elements in Sunday School Growth 31

In 1970, our church had outgrown the Sunday School space we had completed only two years earlier. We badly needed additional nursery and adult departments. Classes were meeting in every available area. In addition to an educational building, the church needed a fellowship hall and family life center. We had enlarged and renovated the sanctuary in 1967. In 1968, we entered a new 45,000-square-foot educational building. Following that, the church built a chapel with additional Sunday School space. As we entered 1970, we realized that we needed additional educational space for the continued growth of the Sunday School.

After prayer and study, the Long Range Planning Committee produced "The Master's Plan." It outlined a challenge to intensify our outreach and build a Sunday School with more than 10,000 enrolled. The deacons received and adopted the report enthusiastically. The church family became excited about the prospect of reaching 10,000 through our Sunday School. The result was a vote to build three buildings: an educational building, a family life center, and a fellowship hall.

The plan was simple and challenging. We would start the educational building, completing two floors and leaving the third floor unfinished until funds were available. Then, we would build a family life center which included a gym, game room, patio, beverage and trophy room, kitchen, and dressing areas for men and women. When this was completed, we would build our fellowship hall and church kitchen.

As we launched this challenging program, the church became very enthusiastic; the income of the church increased dramatically, and Sunday School attendance grew to an all-time high. The result was that we completed the third floor of the educational building that had originally been voted to be left unfinished. The bids on the family life center were unusually low, and this building was completed. All that remained to be built was the fellowship hall. By faith, without any building fund, the church let the contract on the fellowship hall with the agreement that we would give the contractor sufficient notice to stop the project if the building funds were insufficient.

Miraculously, the money came. The fellowship hall was completed! All three buildings were used for Sunday School, and once again, the enrollment and attendance increased.

The church family had a common goal and dream. Starting any project is half the work. A vision gripped our hearts, and a sense of pride and determination motivated us to reach more and more people with the gospel of Christ. Esprit de corps is essential to building a great Sunday School.

Sometimes when we can only see ourselves completing half a project with available and future resources, we begin. We have discovered that in the will of God if we do all we can, God will provide the balance. When a plane passes the midpoint of its flight, it reaches the point of no return. It is closer and easier to go on than turn back. At times, all great Christians and churches reach this point. This is a factor that makes great Sunday Schools.

I am convinced that if a wild, ravenous tiger is loose menacing a community, every ablebodied person will respond to the challenge: "Help us track down the wild tiger!" Conversely, few, if any, will respond to the cry, "Help us trap a vermin-infested mouse!" The challenge to chase a mouse just isn't big enough.

Be careful what you ask for because you might get it. Challenge your Sunday School to do and accomplish great things for God's glory. Do not be satisfied with mediocrity. God is still working miracles. "All things are possible to him that believeth" (Mark 9:23). Would you pray, "Lord, I believe, help thou mine unbelief"? (Mark 9:24).

Witnessing Beyond Your Neighborhood

When I came to Hyde Park Baptist Church as pastor, I observed that most of the members lived within one to three miles of the church. In fact, many of them lived so close that they walked to church. I was happy that the church was reaching the neighborhood, but I was concerned about the city.

Elements in Sunday School Growth

I discovered that the city of Austin had a welcome service that secured the name, address, and phone number of every newcomer who moved to the city. I determined that if the welcome service could visit every newcomer to the city, I could surely visit every newcomer to the city who was either unchurched or a Baptist. Consequently, for more than a decade, six days a week, I made fifteen prospect visits every day, inviting people to come to Hyde Park Baptist Church. When I visited newcomers, I had to visit fifteen families to get one. When I visited people who had visited in our worship services, I could usually visit five families and know for certain that at least one family would join the following Sunday. Often the average was better.

A mathematical factor was established that was sure to work. If I made enough visits, the church would grow. I didn't have to depend on anyone else to visit. If the pastor alone would make enough visits, the church would grow. Naturally, I encouraged the members to visit. We had nights of visitation, weeks of visitation, special visitation emphases, revival visitation, soul-winning visitation, Sunday School visitation, and every other kind of visitation I could promote. But there seemed to be no visits that could take the place of pastoral visits. Often our members would say to me, "Pastor, if you will visit this family, they will join the church." I did, and they joined!

Fifteen years ago, we established a new mission in a growing part of our city. Sunday School growth was slow. I talked with the young mission pastor about visiting prospects. He explained that he was having a difficult time getting his members to visit. The result, he explained, was the the prospects were not being visited.

I asked the young mission pastor how many visiting families he had in church and Sunday School on an average Sunday. He responded, ten or less. I suggested that *he could visit* all ten of those families in two days. *He* was the solution to his visitation problem.

I would say to pastors and church staff members that, if no one else in the church visits, if you visit faithfully and effectively, your visitation alone will probably keep your church growing numerically. It will certainly help you to grow spiritually.

As I discovered that most of the members of our church in 1960 lived very near the church, I resolved that I would set no neighborhood limits on visitation. At that time, the greatest growth in our city was northwest and northeast.

One particular Sunday, a family that lived seven miles away joined our church. One of our finest deacons commented to me, "That family lives in a brand-new section of our city, Northwest Hills. They live seven miles from the church! They live further away than any family in our church!" I explained to that good deacon that *the growth pattern of the city is the opportunity of the church.*

Today Northwest Hills has fifty thousand people living in it. Our church has more members in Northwest Hills than any other church in the city. Some people attend our church from as far as fifty-five miles away. Many people attend our church who live twenty or more miles away.

Remember, *the field is the world.* Do not set limits on God or people to attend church.

Advantages of Distance

There are certain advantages for the church when people drive many miles to come to church. The first and most obvious advantage is that they are coming to their church because they love it. They love it so much that they will drive from their neighborhood to be a part of their church family.

Second, it is obvious that people who will drive five to fifteen miles to church are extremely dedicated. They do not want to go to the church *nearest.* They want to go to the church *dearest.* They are desiring to be spiritually fed and are looking for a Sunday School that will bless their family.

A third advantage is that when church leaders realize that church members drive a number of miles to church, they will begin to compact the church programs. It is absolutely imperative in today's world that we center most of our church programs on

Sunday and Wednesday. For a church to spread its programs throughout all the week, calling families away from their homes and social lives to attend church every night of the week, is a mistake. In fact, it is self-defeating because it reduces church attendance on Sunday and Wednesday.

A key concept in building a great church is the "Sunday-Wednesday concept." Try to group your church meetings on these days. In many churches, committees, mission groups, and music organizations meet on Sunday evening or Wednesday evening before or after services. This will keep meetings short and to the point. It will also encourage worship attendance. Do what is best for you in your situation so that the involvement of church members and visitors is a satisfying experience that helps them grow toward maturity in Christ.

There is another advantage to having your church membership spread throughout the city. You have a great opportunity to reach a whole city for Christ. If you work only in a neighborhood, your opportunity is limited to a neighborhood. But if your members are living throughout the city, you have the challenge of evangelizing the city and, beyond that, even the whole area.

Many of you who read these pages minister in small towns or rural communities. People drive only short distances to church, and you have presently only limited opportunities for reaching beyond your immediate area. In any case, I encourage you to establish a visitation pattern to stay in touch with people. The key to an effective, vital church is relationships between people developed under the leadership of God, not the distance driven to the church facilities. Furthermore, I challenge you to think beyond your own area. As Jesus commanded, think of the world as a mission field.

3
Maintaining a Growing Sunday School
Bob Edd Shotwell

Arthur Flake provided Southern Baptists with five basic principles for maintaining a growing Sunday School. The Flake formula has been followed through the years in Sunday School development. The expansion in recent years of the five growth principles for growth has reinforced what is being done in growing Sunday Schools. The nine principles being promoted now by the Sunday School Department of the Baptist Sunday School Board are being used currently to develop the Sunday School at Hyde Park. These principles can be adapted and used in churches of all denominations which are concerned about growing churches and effective Bible study programs.

Principles should be perpetuated when they are proven valid. Methods of implementation may vary from church to church or from time to time. Churches willing to run the risk of failure in experimenting with new methods will succeed. Fortunately, our church has been blessed with consistent growth. I believe that even a small village church can incorporate some of these principles to strengthen its work. The growth might not always be numerical, but it is real, nevertheless.

These nine principles should guide the Sunday School:
Principle One: Make a commitment to grow.
Principle Two: Identify and enroll prospects.
Principle Three: Expand the organization.
Principle Four: Enlist workers.
Principle Five: Train workers.
Principle Six: Provide adequate space and equipment.
Principle Seven: Conduct weekly workers meetings.

Principle Eight: Promote outreach.
Principle Nine: Teach the Bible to win the lost and develop the saved.

I will discuss all of these principles, but I will not discuss them in the order just listed.

Principle One: Make a Commitment to Grow

The church that definitely and openly commits itself to growth tends to grow. Our church has been committed to growth for many years. This commitment can be seen in the lives of members and ministers.

Develop a Mind-Set for Growth

The proper mind-set for growth in the church must be developed first. This process starts with church leaders—pastor, staff, deacons, committee chairpersons, and Sunday School workers. Believe it or not, every member of the church does not want the church to grow numerically. The status quo is just right for them. It fits them comfortably and gives them a secure feeling of position. New people entering the fellowship threatens many members because they see leadership changing and they feel less known in the membership.

Leaders should seek to bring about the proper meshing of the new members with the old. New talent is needed, but so is the old. Hyde Park has moved from a small neighborhood church to a great metropolitan church. Leadership is shared by long-standing members and new members. Enlist new leaders, but don't lose the members of long standing. Leaders must lead if a church is to move forward.

Another way to develop a growth attitude in the mind-set of a church is regularly to call attention to the Great Commission. Growth is not optional. It is a command. We are to be reaching people with the gospel, to be baptizing the converts, and to be teaching the Bible to the people. Too many churches today appear to be apathetic and lazy about obeying the command from the Lord.

Opinion is divided on the purpose of the church. Many theologians teach that the chief purpose of the church is worship. No one disagrees that, in the fellowship of the church, the members worship. But is this the *chief purpose* of the church?

I believe the chief purpose of the church is to carry out the Great Commission as revealed in Matthew 28:19-20. In the Book of Acts, James stated, "Simeon hath declared how God at the first did visit the Gentiles, to take out of them a people for his name" (15:14).

We best worship Christ as we obey His last command to "make disciples of all nations, baptizing them in the name of the Father and of the Son and of the Holy Spirit, teaching them to observe all things" (Matt. 28:19-20, RSV). Churches develop a mind-set for growth, outreach, and discipleship when they determine that their central task is to carry out the Great Commission.

Almost any church can think of reasons that would limit growth. These may include location, accessibility, declining neighborhood, apartment developments, financial limitations, lack of property, leadership voids, and so on. Hyde Park could have succumbed to these reasons that limit growth. We faced every one of these problems and others. Instead, the church has overcome obstacles to growth and has moved forward to build a dynamic Sunday School and church.

A brother and his older sister were climbing a mountain. The little brother complained about the rocks in his path. The sister enthusiastically responded, "Come on, keep climbing! Those rocks were put there by God for us to use as stepping-stones." That is the spirit we must have as we go forward in building His church.

A third way to develop the proper-mind set is to place priority on Sunday School as the lead organization of the church. Everyone needs to understand that unless the Sunday School grows, everything else is limited in development. The other programs of the church are important and play their unique roles, but the Sunday School is given the responsibility to minister to the greatest number of people at the prime time of the week. Every church member should be in Sunday School and worship on Sunday morning.

The fourth way to develop the proper attitude for growth in the church is to recognize the tremendous spiritual and moral needs of people. People everywhere are in need of the gospel. We need to notice these people and be as concerned about them as we are concerned about neighbors or relatives. This should cause us to want to grow our Sunday Schools and churches. It was a great day in our church when believers saw the multitudes and became concerned enough to do something about it. We saw university students, singles, young marrieds, ethnics, senior adults, preschoolers, youth, and children. We determined with the help of Almighty God to expand until the last lost person has been led to the Savior.

After the mind-set for growth is established, the momentum is present for continued growth. Like a snowball rolling downhill, the more you grow, the more people want to grow. Spirit and fellowship are outgrowths of the growth attitude in the church.

Set Goals for Growth

Study Past Records. If you make a commitment to grow, the next natural step is to set goals in several areas of Sunday School work. In 1967, we made a study of past records to discover pertinent facts about our Sunday School. These facts included:

1. The Sunday School *enrollment* on the first Sunday of October for several previous years. We used only in-house Sunday morning enrollment records and studied the previous five years.

2. The total number of *new members enrolled* in Sunday School in each of the previous five years. In this way, an average number of new members per Sunday can be calculated.

3. The total *number of members dropped* from the Sunday School in each of the previous five years. This can be translated into the average number of drops per week. The difference in enrollment each October minus the number of new members will give the number of drops.

4. The *average attendance in each month* over the previous five years. In this way, attendance trends can be studied, comparing the same months of each year.

5. The *percentage of enrollment present* in each month. It is important to know what percentage of enrollment to expect to be present month by month. We discovered that the *percentage of attendance is constant for a given month* regardless of the enrollment level. This means that *attendance will grow as the enrollment grows* at the expected percentage level that has been established. Attendance will also grow if you can raise the percentage level, but this efficiency rate is very difficult to change in the average Sunday School. Hyde Park's percentage of enrollment to attendance levels are listed below. Do you know your church's level? Yours will probably be similar to ours.

Percentage of Enrollment to Attendance

October	49%	April	46%
November	46%	May	43%
December	39%	June	38%
January	45%	July	38%
February	46%	August	38%
March	48%	September	46%

6. The *record attendance* for a single Sunday. Every church needs to know what its current record is during all its history. How can we project attendance goals if we are not aware of the past achievements? In 1967, our record attendance had been *1,312* over a period of seventy-three years. The current record attendance of *3,249* was set on April 15, 1984.

Set Goals for the Future

After studying the records of the past five years, most goals can be intelligently set. You cannot make real strides forward until you make the commitment and set the goals in several years.

1. *The enrollment of new members is the single most important statistic in the Sunday School* because it controls the progress of the attendance. In setting a goal for new members to be enrolled, we should take into

account the space available to house the maximum enrollment for the organizational structure. For instance, we use a department enrollment ceiling of 12-20 for babies and creepers; 20 for toddlers, twos, and threes; 25 for fours and fives; 30 for grades 1-6; 100-125 for youth; and 125-150 for adults.

In studying our current enrollment potential for our organization and space at Hyde Park, we have discovered that we can enroll 7,045. Our potential by divisions is:

Preschool A (babies, creepers, toddlers)	12 depts.	240
Preschool B (twos and threes)	8 depts.	160
Preschool C (fours and fives)	10 depts.	250
Younger Children (grades 1 & 2)	8 depts.	240
Middle Children (grades 3 & 4)	8 depts.	240
Older Children (grades 5 & 6)	8 depts.	240
Youth (grades 7-12)	6 depts.	750
Singles & Students	8 depts.	2,000
Internationals	3 depts.	400
Young Adults	5 depts.	625
Adults	14 depts.	1,900
Totals	90 depts.	7,045

On October 1, 1983, we had 5,920 enrolled. That meant that we had growth room for *1,125* more Sunday School members. Our immediate goal for new members is to gain *1,125* new members. We have learned that to do this in one year we will need to enroll *2,325* new members because we usually lose 1,200 members per year. It is more realistic, based on past performance, to use two years to reach the full potential; consequently, a goal of *1,750* new members in each of two years will net 500 per year and reach the 7,045 level in two years. Goals by divisions are established as a breakdown of the 1,750. When 7,045 is reached, we need to be prepared to determine the next steps.

2. The increasing of attendance from year to year is urgent. We have learned that *attendance will increase as the enrollment increases at the established percentage rates.* Our goal for attendance then is based on our enrollment projections. For example, if we gain 500 in our

enrollment from one October to the next, we can expect our attendance to go up 245 on the average or 49 percent of 500 in the month of October.

We compare the monthly average attendance with the same month the previous years. This is the only logical way to compare records. It is a mistake to compare October with July. The percentage of attendance to enrollment is higher in October. If you follow this plan, there should always be an optimism in your reporting of Sunday School attendance.

3. *Goals for special high attendance days should be set.* We plan three high attendance days each year. These have become traditional for our people and have been successful. The first high attendance day is on the last Sunday in October to coincide with the Southern Baptist Convention emphasis. The second is on Palm Sunday. The third is the last Sunday of August.

For the Fall High Attendance Day, we set goals in our departments and divisions high enough to reach for an all-time record Sunday School attendance for the church. The department goals should total *more* than the total goal. In October 1983, our goal was *3,100.* We reached *3,114.* Set a goal that is challenging and yet reachable.

On the Spring High Attendance Day on Palm Sunday, every department tries to have the best attendance of the year since the previous October 1. This has always been successful and gives us two great Sundays in a row. Easter Sunday cares for itself with great attendance.

On Summer High Attendance Day, each department seeks to have the best attendance of the summer. The goal for this day is not as high as the fall and spring, but it is set to be a *new record for the summer.* This ends the summer on a high plane and starts the fall on an enthusiastic note.

Principle Two: Identify and Enroll Prospects

If a church is to succeed in building a great Sunday School, it must develop a prospect file of potential members. A rule of

Maintaining a Growing Sunday School

thumb is that this file should be equal in number to the Sunday School enrollment. This can be a card file. Many churches now have their prospects on a computer, enabling them to store the information and then to print out what is needed for outreach. Basically, two simple files are needed in any church. One is a file by families in alphabetical order. Another is a file organized by departments and divisions.

Prospects may be identified in various ways: through newcomer services, visitors in Sunday School and worship services, in-church surveys, resident church members not enrolled in Sunday School, Vacation Bible School, university mailing lists, school profile sheets, day-care information, mothers' day out, and so forth. Churches and associations use people searches extensively to gather information on prospects.

It is doubtful if most churches need to take a census. Usually a great amount of work is expended visiting and typing cards, but there is little follow-up. A church's best prospects are those who visit the church.

After identifying these prospects, the person responsible must do the processing on a weekly basis. This means filing the cards and preparing the information for distribution to the people for visitation. Later, we will discuss the outreach program.

Enrolling people in the Sunday School is the ultimate objective of identifying the prospect. We believe in urging people to enroll the first time they are willing to do so.

When a prospect arrives at our building, we offer information and greeters in four places. The greeters guide people through our buildings to the proper departments. These information stations are places where the proper classification of a person is made. The greeter takes the person to a division station in our building. A worker at the division station places the new person in the proper department after getting all the information on the classification slip.

We try to enroll prospects as new members at the division station and introduce them to the department director as new members. If they do not enroll, we welcome them as visitors. In the Young Adult, Adult, and Singles Departments, the information center takes people straight to the department.

The attitude we show toward new people is of utmost importance. If we are friendly, cordial, and persuasive, a positive impression is made on people whether or not they allow us to enroll them immediately. More than once people have indicated that the church is very friendly, even though it is large.

The Action Program used by many Southern Baptist churches introduced the concept of enrolling people in Sunday School anywhere and anytime they will allow us to do so. Many people will respond to such a friendly, tactful approach and will enroll in the Sunday School. We have enrolled some people by following up with telephone calls when they have visited in our church.

People who join the church can be enrolled in the Sunday School the week after they join. Some churches automatically enroll new church members in the regular departments and send letters to the member and the department and class leadership informing them of their enrollment. For years, our church has automatically enrolled new church members through our New Member Orientation file. Their cards are transferred from this holding file to the proper department file when they attend Sunday School. We do include the New Member Orientation file in our enrollment. If a church does not enroll new members automatically, every effort should be made to get them to enroll the next Sunday.

Our church has a goal to enroll 38 new Sunday School members per Sunday. This will give us *1,976* new members in a year and be more than enough to reach our goal of *500* net gain. Each division has a share of the goal, and results of our enlistment of new members are reported to the people each week on Wednesday night.

Set goals for total new members to be enrolled and publicize them. The net-gain goal is not the one to promote because people tend to forget the attrition factor. In our church, if we make 500 net our goal for new member enrollment, people will forget that we must offset a loss of 1,200 members. We must keep the large goal of total new members before the people. Net gain will occur if we get enough new members to offset the losses.

Prospects are everywhere! Let's find them and do all we can to enroll them in our Sunday School. Christian education and church membership cannot take place until first we locate the prospects and enroll them in Bible study.

Principle Three: Expand the Organization

A proven principle is that *new units grow faster than old ones.* To grow a Sunday School, *new classes and departments are needed.*

Basic Organization

Most churches will have just the basic organization for preschool, children, youth, and adults. Many churches have only two or three preschool departments, one or two children's departments, one youth, and one adult. The sad thing is that many are satisfied with the status quo; consequently, they never add any new classes or departments. This stymies growth.

Even a small church might plan for four preschool departments (babies, toddlers, twos and threes, fours, and fives); two children's departments (grades 1–3 and grades 4–6); one youth department with two classes (junior high, senior high, or boys, girls); and two adult departments (18–39, over 40). This basic organization should be set up regardless of enrollment since the guideline for it would be the developmental stages of the various age levels. Obviously, open country churches with few people and churches in areas with almost no children should adapt these suggestions to meet current and future needs. However, attention should always be given to possibilities for growth.

As the basic organization described begins to reach enrollment ceilings or as needs arise to minister to certain groups, such as singles or language groups, more units should be added. I feel that *a church will never reach singles successfully until it provides a department or class specifically for singles.* New units for preschool, children, or youth may need to be started in order to do a better job of teaching on the level of the member. For example, it is better to have a department for each grade one through six than to mix the grades if ten or twelve members per grade are enrolled. Young marrieds will flourish if they are specifically planned for in the organization. This can be said about any adult group.

Sometimes we hesitate to start new units because we do not have numbers sufficient to do it or because we do not want to shake up the status quo. Our ability to reach people may be waiting on us to start new units targeted for specific groups of persons.

Our records at Hyde Park show the following departmental structure.

Number of Departments & Enrollment

	1960	1970	1980	1984
Preschool	13- 283	14- 304	26- 528	28- 695
Children	9- 326	14- 392	24- 589	24- 598
Youth	4- 156	6- 363	6- 539	6- 690
Adult	10-1018	15-1445	25-3034	30-4196
Totals	36-1783	49-2504	81-4690	88-6179

Without the expansion of the organization to include more departments, we would not have grown as we have. If we still had thirty-six departments, enrollment would be limited to what those departments could handle.

Divisional Organization

As time moved along, we recognized the administrative need to expand our organization beyond the class and department units. The basic four age levels were not sufficient for us in our attempt to administer the program.

Several years ago we set up an organization with eleven divisions in it. Departments are inside the divisions, and classes are inside the departments. Each of our divisions has a director who relates directly to the department directors. Some of these division directors are paid while others are volunteer. Our divisions are as follows:

    Adult (31 & older): 19 departments and 50 classes
    Young Adult (18-30 & married): 6 departments and 16 classes
    Singles & Students (18 & older): 7 departments and 30 classes
    International (18 & older): 4 departments and 21 classes
    Youth (grades 7–12): 6 departments and 34 classes
    Older Children (grades 5 & 6): 8 departments
    Middle Children (grades 3 & 4): 8 departments
    Younger Children (grades 1 & 2): 8 departments
    Preschool C (4's & 5's): 10 departments
    Preschool B (2's & 3's): 8 departments
    Preschool A (Babies, Creepers, Toddlers): 10 departments

By utilizing the division structure, the administrative scope is narrowed and becomes more efficient. The work of outreach and teaching is supervised more closely in the various departments as the division directors are put in place. Not only do we need to add more departments and classes, but we need to streamline our organization to be efficient.

Practical Ways to Begin New Units

1. Move as quickly as possible to a department per year in the preschool and children's age levels. In my opinion, it is better to have a first grade department and a second grade department with three workers and ten children each than to have one department for first and second graders combined with six workers and twenty children. Bible teaching will be targeted better, and growth will result by providing more specifically for a grade level.

2. Provide for career singles separately from college students. If a church targets these groups individually, it will do a better job in reaching and teaching them. A college department can grow quite large in enrollment if enough classes are provided. This is because it has a four-year age span and has a considerable turnover every year. Singles need to have several departments by age levels

or by specific needs. We have found that our Formerly Married Department has met a real need and has grown rapidly.

3. New adult classes can be started by asking a nucleus for the new class to come out of an existing one rather than dividing a class down the middle. The start-a-class plan is a good one as a team of leaders is found to begin a new class. In closely graded departments of two- or three-year spans, classes can be of the same age with the newly formed smaller classes being fed the new members.

4. Entire classes may be asked to move to another department in order to break a bottleneck in the organization. We have found that entire classes will move to the oldest department if they can go as a group.

5. Parallel department age ranges may develop for senior adults. For example, there may be two departments seventy and older rather than one department seventy through seventy-nine and one over eighty. On the older levels, we need to develop compatibility, friendships, and stability that is permanent. These departments need members who are able to drive their cars. If there is a department over eighty, this becomes difficult.

6. Young Adults will respond to a rotation plan where the classes are formed on a yearlong basis, but teachers rotate every three or four months. At the rotation time, a new class can be easily started.

7. Coeducational groupings for adults are with us in great numbers. A coeducational department should have an age span. Class size may be larger since twenty couples means a teacher or outreach leader has twenty contact points. We have started a number of new groupings with a teacher and three or four pairs who volunteered.

At Hyde Park, we have only coeducational classes in our Young Adult Division and Singles and Students Division. In our Adult Division over thirty years of age, we have one track of departments covering all the ages that has only coed classes and a second track of departments covering all ages that has only separate classes for men and women. A choice is made when a person is enrolled as to which track he or she joins.

By following the track system, you can have the best of both worlds. Your Sunday School has classes for couples. It also offers classes for men and women. The ultimate goal is to reach everyone. This system overcomes objections for attending Sunday School.

8. New units can be started for language groups in the Sunday School. Our International Division now has 270 enrolled in four departments. English, Spanish, Chinese (Mandarin and Cantonese), and Korean are used. The departments are structured around the language rather than age spans. Until we began to use the languages in our Bible study, we were not attracting these friends to our Sunday School. We now have twenty-one class units that we did not have eight years ago when this work began.

9. We have successfully used a color-coding system to group people in classes in our Singles and Students Departments. Colored name tags are used for particular classes. When all of one color is used up, new people are placed in a smaller class that still has room.

10. In the Children and Preschool Departments, we have grouped children by geographical location and by regular or irregular attendance factors. We have found this a better way to balance enrollments than by the month of birth.

11. A total restructuring when a new building is built will allow you to bring a new department into existence. Two years from the top end of one department and two from the bottom end of another will make a new four-year department. A complete restructuring is possible by taking all adults and simply placing one hundred people in a department, letting the ages fall according to the years needed to get one hundred people. In our church, married couples stay together in departments based on the younger of the two. This is true when classes are separate or coed.

Principle Four: Enlist Workers

If the organization is going to be expanded, additional workers will need to be enlisted to staff the various departments and classes. The number of workers needed must be ascertained. It is best to set up the ideally staffed organization on paper and then proceed to enlist workers needed. Indeed, enlisting workers is a continuing task even for existing departments and classes. Churches need to be sensitive to those who might be enlisted and trained to serve in the organizational structure.

Ideal Structure

Preschool Departments: Four workers are needed to direct and teach in each department for babies, creepers, toddlers, twos and threes. Five workers are needed to direct and teach in each department for fours and fives.

Children's Departments: Five workers are needed to direct and teach in each department for grades one to six.

Youth Departments: Departmental officers should include a director, outreach director, and secretary. Each class should have a teacher and a student leader.

Adult Departments: Departmental officers should include a director, outreach director, activities leader, and secretary. Each class should have a teacher, outreach leader, activities leader, secretary, and a group leader for every five members.

In addition to this, some churches will have division officers, such as division directors, outreach directors, and secretaries. All churches will have some general officers in the structure.

The ideal number of workers should be sought. This does not mean that you must have the ideal before you can have the new department or class. Obviously, successful Sunday Schools and units within the Sunday School have often begun and functioned without the ideal number of workers.

Methods of Enlisting Workers

In our church, we make a strong effort to give a person only one organizational position. A person thus works *only* in Sunday School, discipleship development, choirs, or mission organizations. This is an excellent plan for any church, but it does take real effort and determination.

Make this a goal toward which you move. Perhaps you cannot accomplish this in one year. If and when you reach this goal, you will find that workers will be more efficient than if they have several jobs.

Discovering potential workers for the Sunday School organization is a never-ending task. All the workers needed are going to come from church membership rolls. Enlist as directors and teachers those who are faithful church members. Study the rolls, asking, Could this person serve if he or she would? A list of possibilities will develop. People should be put on this list only if they have already proven to be faithful in attendance. It is a mistake to put a person in a leadership position who has not been regular in attendance.

Service questionnaires or talent surveys are used successfully to find workers for organizations. This survey is best done in the Adult Sunday School departments on a given Sunday.

Teachers of adults can recommend potential workers from the classes they teach. These are excellent possibilities. As a follow-up, some churches have training classes for potential workers recommended by teachers or who otherwise have expressed an interest in teaching. Potential workers classes will produce a pool of possible workers. These people will have gone through a course of study to prepare them for service. These represent the best possible potential workers.

After figuring the total number of workers needed and making a list of potential workers, plan for actually enlisting workers. In many churches, a nominating committee asks all current workers in the Sunday School whether they would like to continue in those positions for another year. New workers are also enlisted by a nominating or enlistment committee.

In other churches, the nominating committee enlists only the general director and division directors. Then the division directors enlist the department directors who in turn enlist the workers in their own departments.

In yet other churches, the education staff forms the nominating committee and proceeds to work through the process just described. Some current workers are retained; others are asked to shift; others resign, while others are not reenlisted.

The person who leads the group should be the one who does the enlisting. For example the teacher should be enlisted by the director.

A number of churches are now enlisting workers on a permanent basis and only replacing resignations or handling dismissals once a year. This is an acceptable procedure provided a new motivational "send off" for the new year can be planned.

I feel the best way to *enlist new workers is with a personal visit.* At that time, the one doing the enlisting should be honest, forthright, and clear about the responsibility under consideration. We should never leave the impression that a Sunday School job is unimportant, easy, or requires little time. We should ask the person to pray about God's will in regard to a place of service. People can more easily turn us down than God. If God convicts a person of the need to serve, we will have a committed worker. When enlisting a worker, we should offer helps in printed materials or in training courses.

A person being asked to consider a place of service should not be expected to make the final decision at the first contact. Prayer and thought about the place of service should be encouraged. After a few days, we should follow up to get the decision from the person.

Some churches have been successful with enlistment dinners where potential workers are invited to a dinner and are approached about the needs for service. People are asked to indicate their willingness to discuss further the possibility of service. This is followed up by a personal visit concerning a specific job.

Keeping Workers Productive

After workers are enlisted, we are interested in keeping them as productive workers. How do we do that? Here are several suggestions.

1. Be realistic and honest concerning the work in the first place.
2. Enlist properly, making it a matter of prayer and spiritual motivation.
3. Provide training for the task. Conduct regular weekly workers meetings.
4. Provide recognition for workers for the good work they are doing.
5. Help workers gain a sense of achievement by personally complimenting them.
6. Solve problems immediately. Do not let a problem persist.
7. Keep good open communication.
8. Compliment the worker who is faithful, doing a good job, growing a class or department, leading the unsaved to Christ, etc. When you receive compliments regarding your workers, pass them on to the workers.

Additional information on enlisting workers can be found in James W. Chatham, *How to Discover, Enlist, and Train Sunday School Workers* (Nashville: Convention Press, 1982).

Readers will remember that I am discussing the principles in an order that is different from the original list. I now want to move to Principle Eight.

Principle Eight: Promote Outreach

A vital step in growing a Sunday School is to develop a strong outreach program that moves beyond the four walls of the church buildings and into the community. A well-organized prospect file and a great organization staffed by highly trained workers is of little value if the effort is not made to reach out to people not enrolled in Sunday School.

The outreach and group leaders in the Sunday School organization are the key people to make an outreach program really work effectively. We need to enlist and train people for the task of outreach. Training can be given on Sundays during Church Training or Wednesdays at the weekly workers meeting or on the outreach night. It is probably best done on consecutive Wednesday evenings during the workers meetings. Many excellent materials are available for use during these training sessions.

Assignments of prospects for outreach should be done through the Sunday School. From the general officers in charge of outreach, information about prospects would go to the division directors who would pass it on to the departments and subsequently to class leaders. We have found it helpful for our division directors to have the first look at prospects for the initial contact or for assigning names. The greatest danger in this approach is that someone will fail to pass the names to the proper class, teacher, or outreach leader. There is also the very real possibility that after being assigned, no one will visit the prospect. Follow-up is essential in a successful visitation program.

Prospects may be assigned by using the "wholesale" or "retail" methods. "Wholesale" method is to assign prospects in great numbers when the most people are present—namely, Sunday morning at Sunday School. The "retail" method is to assign prospects only to the people who come to the weekly outreach program. Most churches will do some of both. My feeling is that if we assign prospects using the "wholesale" method, we will stimulate some outreach work by people who would never come to a weeknight outreach program. For example, they may see a prospect who lives near them, works in the same building, or belongs to the same club. Those who do participate in a weeknight program can visit the prospects they received on Sunday morning or can secure additional assignments on the outreach night.

I feel strongly that the outreach team of workers in the Sunday

School should be focused on prospective members with the purpose of enrolling them. Already-enrolled members should be contacted on a regular basis by the teachers and officers through the mail, by telephone, or by visit. The temptation we face is to spend our outreach time and energy on enrolled members, neglecting the outreach toward new people who need to be brought into our programs.

A successful way we have found to focus on prospects is to distribute, every Wednesday night, a list of those who visited in our church the previous Sunday. Everyone present at our midweek supper and service receives a list of prospects by areas of our city. We encourage contact with these people before the next Sunday. Prospects will usually receive several contacts from our members, inviting them to Sunday School and worship.

Nothing will take the place of personal visits. Wise church members, however, soon learn they can save hours of time and miles of travel by using the telephone. Many people who visit church or Sunday School do not want church members visiting their homes unannounced. It is good to phone prospects and thank them for visiting Sunday School or church. Ask if it would be convenient for you to visit for ten or fifteen minutes at an agreed-upon date. This shows courtesy and thoughtfulness. It opens the door for a visit. It saves the caller time and travel. Many times a phone call will suffice to enlist the prospect.

The outreach of a church should include going out into the community to establish branch Sunday Schools or Bible classes. They may be started in apartments, in homes, in day-care centers, in housing projects, and in nursing homes. They may be on Sundays or weekdays. These outreach efforts are valuable as extensions of the main church Sunday School. Record their enrollment and attendance separately from the main school to get a clear picture of what is being accomplished in the main Sunday School and in the missions.

Bus ministry has been an important outreach plan for many churches. Some programs have been and remain very active. Others have diminished. In our church, the bus ministry opened our vision to segments of our society which we had never reached before. We sent out buses and brought in people of other races and cultures that our church had never reached before. To be effective, these people must be involved in a good teaching program. Openness to these people has given many of our members a new vision and sense of mission.

As the years have gone by, our bus ministry has turned toward the elderly and the university students, even though we still bring in some children from a black community. Some of these children have been with us all the way to high school graduation. We have been able to lead them to Christ, baptize them, and help them grow spiritually. They are fine Christians today.

All outreach programs need constant scrutiny and evaluation. There may be a better plan, and we need to be looking for it. If your outreach program is not producing results, you may need a change. The continuous Witness Training Program of the Southern Baptist Convention, Evangelism Explosion, or other such programs may be what your church needs to build excitement in evangelism and outreach. The Sunday School outreach program is built into our structure of organization. We have found it most useful.

4
Developing Quality Education
Bob Edd Shotwell

Principle Five: Train Workers

Quality education depends on a number of factors, but probably none is more important than that of trained workers who know how to administer and teach. In our Sunday Schools, we do not have to choose between quality and quantity. We can and should have both. We would be wrong to reach out and bring in people to the Sunday School only to neglect the quality of Bible study. A good quality program will attract people to it. Quality Sunday School work includes a concern for good outreach as well as good teaching. Let's conclude that a great Sunday School will enroll every member it can and will train the staff of workers to the fullest in order to have a quality teaching program.

Jesus trained His workers. In fact, He spent more time training the apostles than He did working with the masses. He knew the rule that it is better to train a few well so they that can multiply their ministry, than to train many directly who are not capable of multiplying themselves by teaching others. We need to follow His example and train our Sunday School leaders who in turn can teach others effectively.

A comprehensive program of training in a church should include an array of opportunities. Let's discuss some of these.

The Church Study Course offered by the Baptist Sunday School Board is an excellent example. Many books are available for study by groups or individually. These books can be purchased through Baptist Book Stores, and titles are found in various catalogs. Leadership Diploma plans are described in a booklet from the Sunday School Board. Transcripts are kept up-to-date by the Board through its computerized record system and are available by using the proper request forms.

Churches can offer study courses on Sunday evenings, Wednesday nights, and special training opportunities on weeknights or Saturdays. Individuals can study courses at home anytime they choose. Associations may offer courses for the workers from the various churches in schools or in the association calendar of training throughout the year with one course offered at a time.

Baptist Telecommunication Network (BTN) is a new training vehicle. The Baptist Sunday School Board broadcasts training materials from Nashville via satellite to be received by churches and associations who prepare to do so. This vehicle could revolutionize our training programs, bringing professional help to the churches without the cost of transporting leaders in person to the local scene. Our leaders at the Sunday School Board prepare materials for broadcast at various times. These materials can be recorded and played to groups at the church when desired. In the coming years, this should become one of our strongest tools in equipping workers. Details concerning costs of equipment and subscription to the service are available from the Baptist Sunday School Board.

Potential worker training classes can be taught during Sunday School, Church Training, and Wednesday evening. A booklet, *Training Potential Sunday School Workers,* by Charles Tidwell, describes this program. The idea is to build up a backlog of trained workers to put into place when needed.

An abundance of training conferences are available through associations, state conventions, and The Sunday School Board at Glorieta and Ridgecrest Conference Centers. It is well worth budgeting the money to send leaders to these various conferences. In addition, a great spirit of fellowship and mission can be generated on such a trip.

On-the-job training is done often in our churches. We enlist people to go to work and then train them while they work. This can be effective if printed materials are given to the workers and if the department and division directors offer help and assistance.

At Hyde Park, we have found that our people respond best to training opportunities on Sunday or Wednesday evenings that are set up for a prescribed period of time. We have also been successful with workshops and conferences set up by divisions. Budget money for training each year. Workers retreats will be helpful. Our Youth Division does this each year with a great response. Part of the expense is covered by the church budget.

If we want quality education, we will need to train the faculty of the school.

Principle Nine: Teach the Bible to Win the Lost and Develop the Saved

Since the textbook of the Sunday School is the Bible, we should diligently teach it to our pupils. We should not teach other materials during Sunday School. This sounds like an unnecessary statement. There are, however, numerous Sunday School classes studying various topics besides the Bible.

There are two ways to study the Bible—one is to build an outline of topics supported by Scripture references; another is to study the Bible book by book and let it speak to the learner's life. Southern Baptists, for example, have curriculum materials available that guide studies either way. These materials are aids to Bible study and are helpful to keep us on a consistent path of study.

Studying the Bible like a history book is not enough. The Bible message of salvation and Christian living needs to be illustrated and applied to the life of the learners. We want our pupils to become Christians who develop into Christlike persons. Christ is our example for living. Application of Scripture is essential if we are to have a quality Sunday School. All of our curriculum aids share some ways of planning and teaching that suggest application procedures.

The plan sheets suggested for the various age groups and the materials in the leadership magazines of the Sunday School Board can be used on Wednesday evenings to prepare the teachers for the application of truth to daily living.

The administration of the Sunday School should select and order the materials that best fit the needs of the church. This is not a decision that should be left to each class. The entire Sunday School needs to be together in its study plan. For example, all adults in the church should follow one of the three curriculum plans. This is the best way to assure the study of the Bible. If every group chooses from material available from many sources, no continuity will exist from one age group to the next, and a group may study something other than the Bible.

Promote Christian Fellowship

One of the great by-products of the Bible-centered quality Sunday School is Christian fellowship. In the New Testament, the church is called the *koinonia* (fellowship). Fellowship is not the main mission of the church but is a by-product of implementing the Great Commission, which is the church's main mission. Sometimes churches limit their outreach because they fear they will lose the fellowship. Sometimes departments and classes do not want to be reorganized because they fear they will lose their fellowship.

Churches with active outreach programs that produce growth have the best fellowship. When a department or class is growing, the fellowship is great! When stagnation sets in, the fellowship is hurt. Introverted Sunday Schools are not as happy as extroverted ones. Sunday Schools are organized to reach out and grow. When that happens, everyone is happier.

Fellowship in a large, growing Sunday School can be enhanced by doing the following:

1. If you have large departments or many first-time visitors, consider using name tags to identify people in all departments above the Youth Division perhaps each Sunday.

2. Coffee, orange juice, or other items can be served just before Sunday School begins. Directors need to begin the large group on

time and should safeguard Bible study time to allow a minimum class period of forty minutes.

3. A monthly social for each adult department is helpful. If not monthly, a quarterly one is a must. An activities leader and committee should be appointed.

4. Division-wide social occasions are good because they provide a larger circle for fellowship.

5. Adult classes are encouraged to have monthly meetings for business and fellowship.

6. Youth and children's departments and divisions should have quarterly socials sponsored by the Sunday School.

7. Dinner clubs inside departments may be organized involving four couples in each group. These would rotate from time to time in order to enlarge the circle of acquaintances and avoid the possibility of an exclusive fellowship group or "clique."

8. Recreation opportunities, such as softball, volleyball, or basketball, will promote fellowship among the participants.

9. Churchwide fellowships, such as homemade ice cream after church on Sunday nights, dinner on the ground, Sunday afternoon picnics followed by an outdoor worship service are possibilities.

As with other suggestions in this book, you will want to adapt these ideas to your own situation.

Evaluate Quality

Evaluation of the quality of Sunday School work is not easy to accomplish. We should try, however, to evaluate the quality of teaching in the Sunday School. Without this evaluation process, we will not know if we are progressing.

Knowledge of Bible content can be done by using tests. These tests may be done anonymously, simply checking the knowledge pupils have over the material studied. A test may be given before a unit begins and the same test given after the unit's study to ascertain progress. The Sunday School Board provides such materials for testing. A general survey of Bible knowledge may be given throughout the Sunday School to see how much people know about the Bible generally.

More important than Bible knowledge is the impact the Bible has made on the lives of the pupils. Evaluation of the spiritual dimension of people is most difficult. We can evaluate our Sunday School by the number of public decisions made by pupils, such as professions of faith, baptisms, special service commitments, or rededications. We can also observe changes in the attitude and conduct of our pupils. Are they more interested in what we are doing in Sunday School now than they were before? Are more people attending than before? Is the class more interested in sharing their faith and soul-winning?

As difficult as it is, we do need to evaluate our work. Where we find weaknesses, we need to improve. At our weekly meetings we should share our evaluations with each other in order to plan for the future.

Principle Six: Provide Adequate Space and Equipment

In order to grow a Sunday School, adequate space must be provided. Space appropriate for preschoolers, children, youth, and adults is necessary. The recommendations I will make regarding space are based on what we have found to be ideal. I believe you should strive for the ideal. However, I also feel you should use what you have. If you are in a small church, new church, or mission setting, I urge you to do the best you can with what you have to teach the Bible. We cannot afford to wait until the circumstances are ideal.

Preschool Departments

Preschool departments should be rectangular in shape and should provide thirty-five square feet per child. If the room is twenty-five feet by thirty-five feet, it will be adequate for twenty-five persons. Of course, it is possible to have good teaching success in space that is not perfect. Preschool rooms should be on the first floor and as close as possible to young adult departments. Rest rooms appropriate to the age of the children should be shared between two rooms. Blue carpet on the floors; vinyl wallpaper in various soft colors such as light yellow, green, or blue; and good lighting from artificial and natural sources make a room very nice and appealing for preschoolers. All departments' rooms should have ample floor to ceiling storage cabinets and in-the-room water available for use. In *Basic Preschool Work*, all equipment needed for preschoolers is described in chapters 13 and 14.

Children's Departments

Children's departments are similar in construction to the preschool rooms, allowing at least twenty-five square feet per person. Tables and chairs of appropriate size are needed to provide four activity centers. The chairs used at the tables may be used for large groups. Ample cabinets are needed for the various programs using the room. Outside light is nice, and good artificial lighting is needed. Rest rooms should be accessible, preferably adjacent to the room. Rooms twenty-five by thirty feet are a good size for grades one through six.

Youth Departments

Youth departments are found in various shapes and sizes. We have two types in our church, both of which work well. The traditional type has a large assembly area with adjoining classrooms designed to seat ten to fifteen. We use this type for grades seven through nine. In grades ten through twelve, we have open rooms with movable partitions. From year to year, the partitions may be set differently to allow for more classes or for a change in the room's configuration. Movable partitions may be sliding on tracks or may be free standing landscape partitions. We have the latter. They seem to work adequately.

Adult Departments

Adults have traditionally used assembly areas with adjoining classrooms for twenty to twenty-five people. If you do not have to use the assembly area for a class, you are fortunate. We have found that our assembly space has been successfully used for classes. We also have been able to make good use of large areas, such as a gymnasium or dining hall, by using movable partitions. You can be creative in determining how space is used. For example, in a dining hall that will seat a thousand at tables, we can have a large college department with three hundred present by using two banquet tables that are hinged together that make a six-feet-tall partition when placed on end. These "table partitions" can be set side by side to divide classes as desired. Adults can successfully use former residences purchased by the church better than other age levels.

Plan for New Buildings

When getting ready to build a new building for Sunday School and Christian education, the planning stage is the most important step. Select an architect who is familiar with the Baptist concept of a Sunday School. If you can find a competent architect who has grown up in a Baptist Sunday School and who is presently attending Sunday School, he or she would be ideal. The architect should design the building to be functional and practical. The cheapest building is probably the most expensive building. Design a building for immediate needs that can be remodeled, expanded, and used to meet the needs of the future.

Before completing the floor plans for the new building, the architect should meet with the Sunday School workers who will be using the space, present the plans, and seek their suggestions. Add to the plans anything they suggest if at all possible. These workers know better than anyone else what the rooms should have and the space requirements. Furthermore, if they give input into the planning of the building, they will be happier when the building is completed and occupied by them and their departments.

Some general suggestions about Sunday School buildings are:
1. If you are in a large church such as ours, it seems wise for all

Developing Quality Education

new buildings to be equipped with television cable and conduits making possible closed-circuit broadcasts.

2. Ample chalk- and tackboards should be provided in rooms and corridors.

3. Enamel paint should be used so the walls can be washed.

4. Directional signs need to be available throughout the facility.

5. Buildings should be of the highest quality, and the best equipment should be purchased. This will save money in the future. We generally get what we pay for.

6. *All* space should be usable for Sunday School. Construction is too costly not to build for Sunday School. Many of the rooms will serve dual purposes. That is, they will also be used for Church Training, the choir program, or perhaps, the mission organizations.

7. Any new buildings should be accompanied by additional parking.

8. Try to make new buildings fit into a master plan. The church should be the most attractive building in the neighborhood. It is generally unwise to erect temporary buildings. They are expensive and have a way of becoming permanent.

9. Plan for adequate landscaping. Use a landscape architect. Install a sprinkler system. Maintain the landscaping.

We have found that we need at least two years to build a new building from the time we begin to develop the plan to occupation. Actually, four years would be more realistic from the time you first begin to discuss the building. If a building reaches its growth potential and you are not ready with new space, then a leveling takes place in your Sunday School growth.

Our experience has been that a new building will generally allow growth in the Sunday School for five years. One way to have your sanctuary full and running over is to build new educational buildings. Reach people for Christ and this will give you the numerical and financial strength for a larger sanctuary. Having done this, you can repeat the cycle again—build the Sunday School—build the worship attendance—build the Sunday School—build the worship attendance.

New people reached will help pay for the new facilities. In our church, in 1983, people gave at the rate of about $22.00 per person per Sunday in Sunday School. This figure includes the total general fund offering and includes money received during the week in the church offerings. One hundred new people in attendance thus produce $2,200.00 per Sunday in new offerings. New space helps produce new people who in turn give more dollars.

Our surveys indicate that 2.75 persons ride in each car to church. Parking spaces close enough to the church to be practical for the people need to be furnished at that rate to handle projected attendance. One hundred parking spaces will handle 275 attendance, and so on. It is difficult for a growing church to have too much parking space. The church could learn from the business world the value of adjacent parking. Visit a shopping center and observe how their parking surrounds the buildings and is adequate and convenient.

A growing church needs the vision to provide space and equipment necessary to continue growth. That church will receive contributions toward construction through fund-raising efforts and also will probably have to borrow money to keep it growing as it builds new buildings. You do not want to be delayed in your goal to reach more people for Christ. If you delay, the cost of construction will escalate. If you delay, people will be lost forever.

Our church is nearly one hundred years old; it was founded in 1894. All current buildings have been constructed since 1950. They are:
    Chapel (former sanctuary) - 1950 - renovated in 1967
    West Education Building - 1957
    East EducationComplex - 1967, 1973, 1974, 1978 (four buildings)
    Christ Chapel - 1970
    Family Life Center - 1974
    Parking Facility - 1981
    Sanctuary - 1983
    Office and Education Building - 1983

From 1967 to 1983, we have built nine buildings and renovated the sanctuary for a total of ten building projects. Without all these buildings, the Sunday School would not have grown to its present level of 6,200 enrolled.

Whatever it takes, we need to keep providing the space and equipment for the growth of Sunday School in quantity and quality.Some have found that rented or borrowed space is possible, while others have successfully used space twice every Sunday.

Principle Seven: Conduct Weekly Workers Meetings

To build a successful Sunday School that reaches people and offers a high quality of teaching, a weekly meeting of workers is needed. This meeting should be one hour long and should include time to discuss administrative tasks, such as records, fellowship plans, training programs, and churchwide programs including stewardship or revivals. Time is needed for planning, reaching, witnessing, ministering activities toward prospects and members. Time is also needed to plan teaching materials and procedures. Materials are organized by units and by Sundays.

Division and department directors are responsible for the enlistment of workers in the sessions and for the program week by week. The various workers may be used to give leadership to the weekly meeting.

A regular schedule needs to be set up and followed to allow the proper time. Included here are several suggestions for Wednesday night workers meeting schedules. Each church needs to fit a schedule to its own situation.

PLAN 1
(for small Sunday Schools)

GENERAL PERIOD (all workers together)   20 minutes
- Administering School Concerns
- Planning for . . . Reaching
     Witnessing

　　　　　　　　　　Ministering
- Praying Together

TEACHING-LEARNING PLANNING PERIOD　　　40 minutes
- All workers together for directed planning of age-group units and lessons (about 30 minutes)
- Special age-group preparation time to prepare room or area of building for Sunday's session (about 10 minutes)

PLAN 2

DEPARTMENT DIRECTORS' PERIOD (meeting in separate room from the supper)　　15 minutes
GENERAL PERIOD (all workers around supper table) 5 minutes
DEPARTMENT PERIOD　　　　　　　　　　55 minutes
- Administering Department Concerns
- Planning for . . . Reaching
　　　　　　　　　Witnessing
　　　　　　　　　Ministering
- Planning Together for Teaching-Learning (30 minutes)
- Praying Together

PLAN 3

GENERAL PERIOD (all workers together)　　10 minutes
DEPARTMENT PERIOD　　　　　　　　　　50 minutes
- Administering Department Concerns
- Planning for . . . Reaching
　　　　　　　　　Witnessing
　　　　　　　　　Ministering
- Planning for Teaching-Learning (30 minutes)
- Praying Together

The schedule that follows is one that Hyde Park Baptist Church has followed on Wednesday nights for ten years with very little change. We are having *850* people for the midweek supper at present, and more people than that are involved in all the various activities.

5:00 - 6:00 - Dinner served in Sanctuary Dining Hall
5:45 - 6:35 - Graded Choirs
6:15 - 7:00 - Reflections
6:35 - 7:30 - Mission Organizations
                Mission Friends
                Girls in Action
                Royal Ambassadors
5:45 - 6:25 - Acteens
6:00 - 6:45 - Midweek Service in Sanctuary Dining Hall
6:45 - 7:45 - Sunday School Workers' Meeting
7:15 - 8:00 - Youth Service in Christ Chapel
7:30 - 9:00 - Sanctuary Choir in Choir Room

You need not wait until everyone can come to the weekly workers meeting to begin. If you wait on that, you will never have one. Simply make plans to begin. Let the program grow and develop. Do not be discouraged. Do not give up.

The results of a good weekly workers meeting are:
1. Better administration week by week.
2. Increased outreach and witnessing.
3. Greater spirit and fellowship.
4. Improved teaching of the Bible.
5. More prayer concern for members and their families.

Many good experiences are possible in the context of active Sunday School classes in a dynamic church. Always in the forefront must be the dual emphasis of teaching the Bible so that what God has done in Christ for our redemption is clear and so that those who are disciples might have a deeper understanding of what it means to be a Christian. The impact of our other efforts is weakened considerably if we fail to maintain the thrust of evangelism and discipleship development. In this ministry the Sunday School supports, and is supported by, other church program organizations and other activities which reach out to touch the lives of people and to grow and develop strong churches.

5
Varied Ministries Contributing to Growth
Bob Edd Shotwell

In a dynamic church there are other ministries that can be outreach tools in bringing people into the Sunday School and church. Some of these programs are conducted during weekdays, utilizing building space that would otherwise be empty of people.

Recreation Programs

A church can and should develop a well-rounded program of recreation. This kind of ministry will result in the involvement of many people who might not be reached by the traditional types of programs. Remember in the New Testament, one name for church is *koinonia* or fellowship. Churches should pray together and also play together.

Recreation can range all the way from participation on teams in leagues, such as tennis, golf, or running to aerobic classes, to family outings, to trips, to departmental socials, to camps, and so forth.

Persons may be involved in the recreation ministry as their first contact with the church. Then, they may be enlisted in the Sunday School. Some leagues require Sunday School attendance for participation. Some recreation ministries sign in all participants, accumulating prospects for Sunday School.

We have discovered that our Sunday School departments benefit greatly from fellowship activities on Friday evenings when we provide a meal and games.

Any church can have a recreation ministry whether it has a recreation building or a paid staff. Some very successful programs have operated with a volunteer structure.

Senior Adult Programs

As an outgrowth of Sunday School, but also as an outreach endeavor, a multifaceted senior adult ministry can be started in almost every church. This ministry can include recreation, crafts, or program features. Trips to interesting places can be planned for senior adults. Retreats and camps may be held; twice a year has worked for us. Many of our Baptist camps now provide for adults in special facilities.

Seminars especially designed for senior adults may be offered in Church Training. A meals program can be provided for homebound persons once or twice a week. Churches serving Wednesday meals could take these to homebound members. Homebound ministries in nursing homes or in private homes may be part of this ministry. Transportation provisions may be made on Sundays and weekdays. Some churches have entered into housing provisions for senior adults.

All of these various programs are extra to the regular Sunday School work and should be outreach vehicles for the Sunday School.

Weekday Bible Studies

In recent years, many Bible study groups have formed outside the regular church program. If these groups are sponsored by the local church, they can be a great outreach arm for the Sunday School and an added opportunity for people to study the Bible.

These classes are conducted in homes, nursing homes, fire stations, and churches. A number of churches are having successful men's and ladies' luncheons with Bible study as part of the program. These may be in the church dining room or in a location in a business district.

Prospects for Sunday School may be located in these Bible study groups. These people may have been brought by church members to weekday classes.

Child Development Center

Many churches have provided weekday child-care programs. We have found this to be an important outreach program for the Sunday School and Vacation Bible School. Parents and children who come to a church building every weekday can be invited to also come on Sundays.

Biographical information on each child can help determine those who are prospects for the Sunday School. This information can be passed on to the proper Sunday School department for visitation and follow-up.

Even if a family is never reached for Sunday School, the church has a great opportunity to teach the child during the week. A good efficient day-care program puts the church in a position to teach and minister to many children and families not reached in any other way.

The Christian School

The Christian school with grades kindergarten through twelve opens the door to an extended Bible teaching ministry every day, as well as providing an opportunity for outreach to students and parents for the Sunday School. More and more schools are being started in churches. Some have grown to an enrollment of one thousand or more. Imagine the value of Christian education in all subjects and the value of Bible study on a daily basis in the classroom. Churches which have schools will attest to the fact that it is not easy to become involved in this ministry, but the positive results far outweigh the negative difficulties.

An elementary school is more easily started and operated than a high school. In elementary school, children can remain in the same classroom. The unit is operated by one teacher and is self-contained. A good plan is to begin one new grade each year. For example, year one you would have only kindergarten. Year two, you would add first grade, and so on. This is the method we followed. Today we have nearly one thousand students in our Hyde Park School System (kindergarten through grade twelve).

Camps and Retreats

One area of outreach to help the Sunday School is the camping program of the church. Youth camps and retreats reach out to unsaved and unenlisted youth like few other programs. Imagine a youth camp with 250 to 350 or even 550 to 600 participants, many of whom can be reached for Christ and the Sunday School. Overnight Retreats can be valuable assets to the Sunday School.

Singles will also participate in great numbers in camps and retreats. Labor Day weekend is a good time for single adults and college students to have a retreat.

Follow-up is necessary to enjoy the fruit of the labors involved in a camping program. Prospects for the Sunday School need to be enlisted immediately. New converts from the camps need to be baptized as soon as proper follow-up is done. If permission of the parents can be secured, it is inspiring to baptize new converts the last day of camp at camp. Perhaps this can be done in a river, lake, or creek. An outdoor baptismal service is inspiring.

Sunday School and Other Program Organizations

The varied ministries of a church provide prospects for the Sunday School. Leaders and participants in these activities should be alert to the possibilities for enlisting people in Sunday School. Those who might be involved in recreation or other programs but not Bible study should be given the opportunity to enroll in Sunday School. On the other hand, Sunday School leaders have an excellent opportunity to encourage involvement in other church program organizations. Many who are active in Sunday School do not attend training programs, mission organizations, music activities, or other ongoing programs. Sunday School department directors, teachers, and members should urge participation to strengthen personal growth and to support the other activities. A growing Sunday School is a ready-made "prospect file" for other church program organizations. Activities should seek to be mutually supportive. A growing Sunday School should mean that all phases of the life and ministry of the church are growing.

6
Challenges that Make a Great Sunday School
Ralph M. Smith

Are you really satisfied with your church as it is today? If you are, you are in trouble, for to be totally content is to have no unfulfilled dreams for your church. You need to accept the challenge to make your church all God would have it to become. It takes guts to leave the ruts.

Dare to dream of your church being filled with God's Holy Spirit. Seek God with your whole heart. Pray for more dedicated Christian teachers, directors, and church members. Where do you begin? The pessimist announces: "I've got to see it before I believe it!" No, you've got to believe it before you see it! Jesus said, "Blessed are they that have not seen, and yet believe" (John 20:29). "All things are possible to him that believeth," promised our Lord! (Mark 9:23). The dream precedes the scheme!

Here are some challenges that could weaken a Sunday School and church. But challenges stretch us and help us to grow. Every problem is a potential opportunity. There are no projects unless there are problems, no forward movement without friction. The psalmist said it beautifully: "When they walk through the Valley of Weeping it will become a place of springs where pools of blessing and refreshment collect after rains!" (84:5-6, TLB).

Challenges have a way of coloring a church, so *you* pick the color. Don't be dull and drab; be bright as the sunshine of God's promises.

Centering on the Individual

One of the first challenges a growing church faces is depersonalization. As the organizations within the church begin to grow numerically, some of the "old" members begin to feel left out. These former faithful members may become irregular in attendance. Sometimes they visit and/or join other churches. They no longer feel needed. Members of a growing church may develop a feeling they are being depersonalized.

Dynamic, growing churches today are most adequately fulfilling personal needs. Adults who will not attend a Sunday School class of forty may gladly attend a class of ten where they feel they count as individuals. In an age of depersonalization, it is imperative that the church keep its emphasis on the individual. One key way for a church to establish and maintain this emphasis is through quality Bible study and fellowship in Sunday School classes.

Often individuals can be given responsibilities and offices in the Sunday School that keep them from feeling depersonalized. It is important to have a class president, secretary, outreach leader, and social leader. This gives individuals an opportunity to contribute to as well as receive from the Sunday School. It strengthens the person and the program.

When Sunday School members are absent, they should be contacted. Letters are good. A phone call is better. A personal visit is the best.

Years ago, when our Sunday School was small, I systematically visited every person on the Sunday School roll who was not a member of the church. One Saturday, I visited the home of a teenager who was enrolled in Sunday School but unsaved. The mother warmly welcomed me into their home. After a while, I asked to talk with her son. She began to weep. Then she informed me that he was in jail. I talked with her, prayed with her, and encouraged her. I promised to visit her son. I was brokenhearted as I left the home. For no one in his Sunday School class had called or visited during the past six months.

The business world is rediscovering the importance of the individual. It remains to be seen whether the church can read the signs of the times. Churches make a sad mistake if they think more adequate buildings can substitute for individual concern. Legion are the congregations which have felt that a new church building would inspire great increase in attendance. No house of worship or Sunday School building, no matter how attractive, can take the place of love and fellowship. The congregation that is depending largely upon a building to increase attendance will be sadly disappointed. Church buildings are only tools in God's harvest field. They can be an important factor in the growth of a congregation. However, buildings alone will not build a congregation.

Individuals must be sought purely for their own sakes by those who have the concern of Christ. We must not seek people to increase our numbers or to extend the influence of our churches. The ground rule in visiting prospects should be courtesy, friendliness, kindness, and love. Visit in such a way that the prospect knows that he or she is important to you and your church. Visit in such a way that the door is left open for a return visit.

Placing the Kingdom Above the Institution

The growing church must be careful that its primary function not become the service of itself rather than the gospel of Christ. Institutionalism reflects an excessive dependence upon institutions with overtones of standardization and regimentation.

The New Testament breathes the spirit of freedom, which is the very opposite of conventionality and/or regimentation. Paul informed the Corinthians that "where the Spirit of the Lord is, there is freedom" (2 Cor. 3:17, RSV). The ministry of Jesus breathes an atmosphere of religious freedom (Mark 7:1-7).

Institutionalism may be reflected in a church's visitation program. One minister said, "We don't bother with university students, since they will be here temporarily and not be of any help to our church." By way of contrast, another congregation in a great seaport keeps in touch with servicemen moving in and out of their community. Another church in a college city does minister to students. Perhaps this church doesn't show a great increase over a ten-year period, but it has a tremendous ministry for Christ in a transient area. Here is a church that is seeking first the kingdom of God (Matt. 6:33).

Do not ever think that when a member moves away, you are losing a member. Although it is true that the attendance may drop, you should think of this member as a potential worker in another church. Be grateful that you had a part in this member's preparation for further service.

Sometimes we have a "too-busy-to-evangelize" attitude. In order to counteract this attitude in our congregation, every Wednesday night we give the names of all people who visited either the Sunday School or church to members and ask them to contact the visitors during the week. Nothing the church does is more important than evangelism.

Church members are sometimes judged by the number of church services they attend. We must balance the "come-to-church" emphasis by a "go-and-witness" thrust. "Enter to worship, depart to serve" has become cliché for many churches. We need to make this a statement of congregational practice and not simply something printed on our orders of worship.

An increasing number of congregations today are placing great stress upon individuals scattering to witness for Jesus Christ. As members see themselves doing the work of Christ in the community, a sense of purpose pervades the life of the congregation.

Multiplying Classes

If a Sunday School is to grow and be effective, classes must multiply constantly. Small classes are especially important for children and preschoolers. Children from underprivileged areas may require an even lower teacher-student ratio.

Generally new classes grow faster than old ones. When one class can become two or two classes can become three, several good things happen. A new teacher is enlisted to go to work for God. The classes are all challenged to reach new members. The Sunday School is dynamic and alive with growth. New excitement is generated in the department. It should also be added that, in the same way, new departments can be created.

I believe it's generally better to take two classes and create a third class. This is, in most cases, preferable to dividing one class in half. Remember, the heartbeat of Sunday School is evangelism and outreach.

Since the multiplication of classes requires the multiplication of teachers, the bottleneck often comes at this point. Many congregations are short of teachers. Many Sunday Schools are not training teachers in large numbers because they have never organized to train teachers. There is a gift to teaching that is given by the Holy Spirit. But many adults in Sunday School classes have not been asked to teach, enrolled in classes that will prepare them to teach, or challenged with the idea of teaching. These adults need to be enlisted privately and challenged publicly to become teachers.

Adults who are asked to teach sometimes reply, "Thank you, but I do not feel I know enough about the Bible to be a teacher." Undoubtedly, they are very sincere in their answer. Perhaps they are underestimating their knowledge of the Bible. Many Christian adults have attended at least three church meetings totaling four hours of worship and teaching each week. Additionally, many have attended other worship services, evangelistic services, and special meetings. By the time these adults are forty, they could have been in a total of 8,320 hours of religious services. By contrast, the university student graduating after four years has spent 2,176 hours in the classroom.

It is difficult to believe that an individual of average intelligence with a total of over 8,000 hours in religious services is incapable of teaching someone else at least the fundamentals of the Christian faith. Additionally, all kinds of wonderful Sunday School helps are available today for willing teachers. We must do a better job of encouraging and enlisting prospective teachers. This is the essential step if we desire to multiply classes.

Prospective Sunday School teachers do well to remember the words of Ralph Waldo Emerson: "Always take a job that's too big for you, and then do your best." Teachers also have the blessing of the Holy Spirit's help.

Beyond the multiplication of classes, we desperately need to multiply Sunday Schools. One expert in Sunday School growth said, "We need 50,000 new congregations in the US and Canada—tomorrow!" In 1790, the nation was approximately 20 percent urban and 80 percent rural. Today, these figures are reversed. The establishment of new Sunday Schools and congregations in urban areas has not kept pace with the rate of urbanization. This constitutes one of the great challenges given to the Sunday School in today's world.

Overcoming Declining Attendance

What can you do when your Sunday School is experiencing a decline in attendance? Step 1 in solving any church problem is to pray. Lay the problem before the Lord. Seek His leadership, help, and solution.

Step 2 is to remember the basic principle that attendance *follows enrollment*. The important statistic in the Sunday School is *Sunday School enrollment*. If you can find ways to increase your enrollment, your declining attendance problem will be stopped. Indeed, you will experience an increased attendance.

Do not seek to make an excuse for declining attendance. It is easy to rationalize away the problem. There is, however, no easy analysis for declining attendance. Perhaps the greatest reason for declining Sunday School attendance is a subtle shift in the past two decades from evangelism to education. Southern Baptists built the largest denomination in America on the motto: "The Sunday School is the evangelistic arm of the church."

A Sunday School teacher with a desire to win the lost to Christ will produce a growing class. The class goal must always be to assist the new convert to "grow in grace, and in the knowledge of our Lord and Saviour Jesus Christ" (2 Pet. 3:18). List the churches that are growing great Sunday Schools, and you will find that evangelism is the primary purpose. This is why they are growing.

Challenges that Make a Great Sunday School 81

Their methods may differ, but their mandate is unmistakable. Like the Savior, they are trying "to seek and to save that which was lost" (Luke 19:10).

Years ago, it was said that "85 percent of all who join the church come from the Sunday School." Today, most who join Sunday School come from the morning worship services. Seldom do people join the Sunday School who have not first visited the morning worship services and decided they are inspired by the music and blessed by the fellowship and spiritually fed by the pastor's sermon. Consequently, that which takes place in the morning worship services can greatly help or greatly hinder Sunday School attendance.

Two of the key people responsible for Sunday School growth (or lack of it) are the pastor and minister of music. If visitors in your church are blessed spiritually by the worship service, you have an open door to enlist them in your Sunday School. It is doubtful that any amount of visitation or promotion can overcome consistently weak sermons and music.

The wise Bible writer stated, "Where there is no vision, the people perish" (Prov. 29:18). Lack of vision kills churches. Churches stop growing and being effective when they cease to provide expanded facilities and expanded staff.

Sin can take the vitality from a Sunday School. The growth of the church can be stunted when sin, regardless of its form, invades and disrupts the fellowship. Even subtle sins can hurt Sunday School attendance. Deacons, for example, should remember that they are ordained to maintain the peace and harmony of the church (see Acts 6).

When the standards of Sunday School workers are broadened, and separation from sin is minimized, God takes the spiritual power away from the teachers. Sin ultimately takes away a Sunday School teacher's incentive to evangelize the neighborhood. A book could be written on this subject, but I believe all of us could agree that our basic problem is always sin.

The words of this paragraph are going to be difficult for some to believe, but read them carefully because thirty years of experience have proved this to be true in my own life. The employment of wrong principles and methods can kill the church.

A ripe illustration of this is the idea that "quality leads to quantity," that is, the good church will be a growing church. The truth, however, is there is no cause and effect relationship between *quality and quantity*. I have seen outstanding churches that have not grown during the past twenty years. Their quality was superb. By the same token, I know of some churches which thrive on gimmicks and grow on promotion, yet the results are disastrous when the Word of God is not rightly taught.

God wants us to have the best quality we can have. I personally am opposed to using gimmicks. We must be careful, however, to form the belief that if we have good quality, the churches will grow automatically. We must also be careful not to use cheap tricks and gimmicks to get people to church and, when they arrive, have nothing to feed them.

Reaching the Youngest and Oldest

If a Sunday School is to please our Lord, it must reach the youngest baby and the oldest adult. How else can we carry out Christ's mandate to "Go ye into all the world, and preach the gospel to every creature" (Mark 16:15)?

A Sunday School gets its enthusiasm from its young adults, it gets its teachers and leaders from its adults, and it gets much of its money from those fifty-five to sixty-five years of age. A Sunday School *gives* its love through its ministry in the preschool division and its care of senior adults. These are the ones who have just come from heaven and are the nearest to heaven. These are the groups to whom we can give. It is indeed more blessed to give than to receive.

Every age in the Sunday School is important and critical. All people are important in the eyes of God. Jesus, however, seemed to have a special love for children. He said, "Suffer little children, and forbid them not, to come unto me: for of such is the kingdom of heaven" (Matt. 19:14). Perhaps the preschool is the most important division in the Sunday School. No one is ever taller than when he or she kneels to help a child. That is when you are closest to heaven.

I believe the preschool is the most important of all divisions in the Sunday School. Jesus said, "Take heed that ye despise not one of these little ones; for I say unto you, That in heaven their angels do always behold the face of my Father which is in heaven. . . . Even so it is not the will of your Father which is in heaven, that one of these little ones should perish" (Matt. 18:10-14).

Make your preschool division a showplace of the church. Spare no expense in making the rooms clean, bright, and beautiful.

Seek out the most dedicated workers for these departments. Try to enlist as many men as women to work with the babies, creepers, and toddlers. Make the reception area attractive. Have several men and women in the reception area to greet new parents who bring their children to church for the first time.

Encourage parents to come to Sunday School, to church, to the activities of the church, and to *bring their preschoolers*. Assure the parents that the preschool teachers will take good and faithful care of their children while they attend programs that interest them. Our church never has meetings when the preschool departments are not open. We want to enlist the whole family, beginning with the youngest baby.

When my wife and I moved to Fort Worth, Texas, to attend seminary, we had a six-month-old daughter. We visited Travis Avenue Baptist Church the first Sunday after we moved to the city. The preschool directors were friendly, courteous, and loving. They made us feel that our daughter was the most important child in the world. The rooms were spotless and well staffed. We were given complete assurance that our daughter would be taken care of by loving hands.

You would know the baby department won our hearts. We loved the Sunday School class we attended that Sunday. The preaching was biblical and Spirit filled. The music was inspiring.

The second Sunday, we again went to Travis Avenue Baptist Church and joined. Regardless of all the great qualities of that great church, we would have joined just because of the baby department. We were infinitely more concerned about our daughter than about ourselves.

I believe we were a normal young couple. If you want God to bless your Sunday School, give central attention to your preschool departments. If you want your church to be filled with young adults, major on the nursery. Spare no effort or expense to make them cleaner, brighter, and more efficient than any hospital.

Some guidelines that we follow in our preschool area. Perhaps you can use some or all of these ideas in your church.

Help Your Baby at Church!

1. Label *all* of his possessions: diapers, pacifier, bag, clothes, bottles, etc.
2. Please bring these in bag:
   change of clothes
   pacifier (if needed)
   light blanket for babies
   bottles with name on them
   plenty of diapers
3. If baby has special instructions, please clip instructions on outside of bag.
4. Medication must be given by parent.
5. Please do not bring toys to church.
6. Always complete instructions on clipboard for your child's Sunday School room.
7. If breast fed, have water or juice in bottle for child.
8. Formula must be ready to give to child.
9. Please do not bring solid food unless already prepared and in an infafeeder.
10. The church provides crackers for creepers and toddlers.

If there is any group that needs a Sunday School and the Sunday

School needs, that group is the senior adult.

These senior adults have more time to give to the church than any other group. By reason of their maturity and experience, they are often our wisest counselors. Beyond a doubt, senior adults are some of our best prayer warriors. They are uninhibited and open. They are honest and forthright. They are creative and willing. Often they are the most faithful members of the Sunday School.

As America grows older, the church of tomorrow will take seriously the outreach possibilities among senior adults. There are approximately 23 million older adults today, and there are 30 million predicted by the year 2000.

Unique methods are essential in reaching older adults. Most older adults believe in God; however, many are unchurched. What methods can our churches employ to reach, enlist, win, and train senior adults?

First, church members need to be conscious that older adults are in their midst. A word needs to be said now and then to encourage the church to think about the needs of senior adults. Failure to do this results in their needs being bypassed for the needs of young adults, teenagers, university students, and others.

Second, senior adults are very capable of ministering to their own and others in the church family. A program designed to minister to senior adults is not enough. Senior adults need to be challenged to be leaders in the church, teach, chair committees, and set high standards for younger Christians.

At the same time, younger church members must remember that older adults, especially the very old, need people to minister to them. Often, transportation is a problem. At times they need counseling and referral help, as well as financial help.

Churches that care for the physical needs of senior adults find that they are caring for spiritual needs. For example, some senior adults are no longer able to drive because of physical problems. Unless transportation is provided for these people, their physical problem becomes a spiritual problem. They may begin to feel that the church no longer cares for them.

Some years ago, our church purchased a van. It is used each Sunday to pick up senior adults and bring them to Sunday School and worship services. Some are unable to stay for both, so the van makes several trips to meet the individual needs of our senior adults. We also have an agreement with the cab company that we will pay the taxi fare of any senior adult brought to church on Sunday morning. Other members then take the senior adults home after the service. Additionally, we tell our senior adults to phone the church anytime they need transportation to shop, go to the doctor, or attend any church meeting. We have a dedicated layperson who uses the church van to perform this service. In any outreach program, transportation is important.

Churches can also help meet the needs of senior adults who have hearing problems. As we grow older, our hearing ability diminishes. Recently, our Senior Adult Department moved to a new assembly room. They immediately asked for a speaker system. At first, I felt the request unreasonable. Then I realized that many of them used hearing aids and most of the others have reduced hearing ability. By the second Sunday they were in their new department, a new speaker system had been installed. We have a commitment to do everything we can to take care of the senior adults.

Special considerations are very important in meeting the needs of senior adults. Their meeting rooms should be very close to the sanctuary. Rooms on the ground floor level or with very few steps are preferable.

Senior adult classes should be a mixed age group. This will give each class some members who are able to drive. Do not grade the classes 65-68, 69-72, 73-79, 80 and up. The oldest class will have a great disadvantage in the number of those active enough to minister and chauffeur others to church, meetings, and parties.

Here are some suggestions for ministering to senior adults.

1. Plan bus trips with senior adults, inviting prospects. A one day or three day (two night) trip is preferable. This is the only way some senior adults will be able to travel.

2. A one-morning-a-week senior adult program. Here they can meet, enjoy fellowship, and play games. Our senior citizens group meets on Thursday in our senior adult center. It was formerly a dance studio. The senior adults renovated the building themselves. Once a month, they have a covered dish luncheon. On the other Thursdays, they have coffee, tea, soft drinks, cake and enjoy games, fellowship, and crafts.

3. Have a good hospital visitation program. This means more to senior adults than almost any other ministry we perform. By reason of their age, they are often hospitalized. They need someone from the church to visit, speak an encouraging word, and have a prayer with them.

4. Each church should have an effective bereavement ministry. Senior adults lose friends and family members, and the families of seniors lose parents and loved ones. A strong ministry of support is essential.

5. Many senior adults need referral help. The church should be prepared to recommend lawyers, doctors, counselors, and social security help.

Equipping Others to Minister

Is the primary function of the Sunday School only leading people to know Christ as Savior and then teaching them the doctrines of the faith? If understood like this, the philosophy falls short of the New Testament concept of *disciple.* Jesus our Savior chose twelve disciples. He not only called them to salvation and taught them doctrine but He also equipped them to minister to others. He said, "As my Father hath sent me, even so send I you" (John 20:21).

A primary function of the Sunday School is to equip people in such a way that they are able to minister to others. Thousands of congregations have members who have been faithfully attending as pupils for twenty, thirty, and forty years. The thought seldom occurs to the teachers or the pupils that the purpose of the school is to produce teachers of others. Paul reminded Timothy that he was to pass on the teaching that he had received (2 Tim. 2:2). In chapter 5, the writer of Hebrews was distressed because his readers had not grown to be teachers (v. 12). Adult Sunday School classes are filled with hundreds of thousands of potential teachers who have yet to teach their first lesson.

The apostle Paul left very little doubt about the primary role of those who function as leaders in the church. They are to equip the saints for ministry (Eph. 4:11-12). It is unfortunate that many translations have a comma that separates "saints" from "the work of the ministry." This misplaced punctuation has sometimes been referred to as the "fatal comma." When the comma is removed as in this translation, the passage reads, "His gifts were that some should be apostles, some prophets, some evangelists, some pastors and teachers, to equip the saints for the work of ministry" (Eph. 4:11-12, RSV). The work of Christian leadership is then clearly defined as preparing the people of God to minister.

This should be one of the goals of every Sunday School teacher or departmental director. Sunday School members should be reminded that they are being taught so they in turn can teach others. The Sunday School is ministering to them with the purpose in view that, ultimately, they will become ministers themselves.

Though a church has but one pastor, it has many ministers. Each member of the congregation should be a minister of the gospel of Christ. A fundamental error permeating many churches is related to the scope of the leadership of the pastor. "The minister" is employed primarily to minister to the congregation. His salary comes from the congregation. The members of the congregation have certain expectations of the minister, most of which are related to the spiritual needs of the congregation. It is true that the pastor should be a minister. It is equally true that the Sunday School should seek to equip every member to visit the sick, teach the Bible, win the lost, and call upon other members of the congregation as they need help.

A Sunday School challenged with the concept that every member is a potential leader will have an abundance of directors, teachers, and workers. When this concept of equipping others to minister does not permeate the Sunday School, there is inevitably a shortage of directors, teachers, and workers.

No organization rises higher than its leadership. A Sunday School that is not continually producing new leaders who are equipped to minister will find that its physical, numerical, and spiritual growth is hindered. The Sunday School should equip others to minister.

Every Problem an Opportunity

I believe that every problem we face in building and maintaining a Sunday School can be turned into a glorious opportunity. Wallace E. Johnson, cofounder of Holiday Inns of America, Inc., once said to me, "If someone hands you a lemon, squeeze it real hard, add sugar, and you can turn it into a lemonade." I have followed his advice, and it works!

When you seem to be getting bogged down in growing, maintaining, and building your Sunday School, remember that every problem is a potential opportunity. Jesus our Lord took the cross of His crucifixion and made it the means of our salvation. He conquered death by His glorious resurrection. Paul, the apostle, has assured us that we are "more than conquerors."

A Problem Teacher

What do you do when you have a problem teacher in your Sunday School? Some church leaders lose a lot of sleep and perhaps even get an ulcer. After all, why pray when you can worry? Why solve the problem when you can talk about it, brood over it, and worry about it for days and weeks on end? Seriously, even this problem is an opportunity.

Consider one of the following suggestions:

1. Whatever method of approach you use, begin with prayer. Jesus has taught us that we should pray that the Lord of the harvest will send forth laborers into His harvest. Sometimes we should pray that the Lord will take some of our laborers and

encourage them to assume other responsibilities or even be a member of a class.

2. Talk with the teacher and ask if he or she is happy teaching. Often, you'll find the teacher will say, "No, this is really not my gift."

3. Ask the teacher if he or she would consider becoming a departmental superintendent, outreach leader, social chairman, or whatever his or her particular gift might be.

4. Consider asking the teacher to move into a different area of the Sunday School. Some people who are weak adult teachers make excellent preschool teachers. Conversely, some teachers who cannot relate to children are excellent with college students. Sometimes our workers are the proverbial square pegs in round holes. We need to help them to find their unique places of service. There is a spiritual gift of teaching.

Additional Space

There are few things that will so quickly slow down or stop the growth of a Sunday School as inadequate space. What do you do when you know that you need additional space?

Remember that the members of our churches are very discerning. Generally speaking, they are dedicated Christian people. When their classes and departments begin to get crowded, they sense the need for additional buildings. In casual conversations, talk with them about the need of the church for additional educational space. Talking with the teachers and directors in the departments where additional space is a necessity is particularly helpful.

The second step is to meet with the proper committee or committees in the church and lay before them the statistical growth of the Sunday School. Better still, present to them the challenge the Sunday School faces. Encourage them to consider building additional Sunday School space.

We have found that a long-range planning committee is most helpful. Ask the deacons to recommend to the church that a long-range planning committee be appointed to study the future of the church. This study should not only encompass buildings but also programs, ministries, budgets, and goals for the future. Give the committee ample time to study and bring back a report to the church family. Included in the report might be a recommendation to build not one but several new buildings.

A Church in Decline

One of the greatest challenges a church will ever face is decline in membership, Sunday School enrollment, Sunday School attendance, church attendance that has happened over a period of ten to twenty years. How can this trend be reversed? This is a great problem, but it affords leadership a tremendous opportunity. In this section, I want to bring together some elements mentioned earlier and expand some of the ideas I feel can be helpful to churches.

For a church in decline, the first step in reversing the trend is a vision in the heart of the pastor which is manifested in the pulpit. Seldom are we defeated from the outside until we are first defeated from the inside. When a pastor has a vision of what the church can become and the people begin to sense his optimistic spirit through the sermons he preaches in the pulpit, the church is on its way to a new spurt in growth.

As new people are enlisted in the church, put them in *new* Sunday School classes and departments. Generally, new units grow faster than old units. Start a new class or department for singles, another for the young marrieds, and a third for young adults. Work diligently with the leadership of these new units; for from these, growth will come.

The next step is to improve the facilities you have. A fresh coat of paint on the outside of the church building can make it more inviting. New landscaping will enhance the entire church plant. Department by department, renovate the educational buildings. Put new carpet on the floor. Change the lighting fixtures. Do everything you can to upgrade the facilities. This step will be costly, but it will pay big dividends.

Begin an aggressive advertising campaign. In a large metropolitan area, churches that once were prominent can become unknown. Budget is a limiting factor, but use the city newspaper, radio, and perhaps even television. Mail services will furnish labels for your immediate area. Produce a beautiful brochure advertising the ministries of the church, and mail one of these to every household within three to five miles of your church.

Begin an aggressive visitation program. The best prospects you have are those who visit the worship services or Sunday School. Make certain that each visitor is phoned, written a letter, or personally visited within a week after visiting your church. Visit with the idea of enlisting them in the program organizations of your church. Ask them to become members of your congregation.

In all of our work, prayer is our ultimate power. Prayer links us to heaven. When we organize, we see what people can do. When we pray, we see what God can do. Ask God specifically to help you grow a great Sunday School. Before God, ask for specific numbers of people to join the Sunday School each week. God from the throne of grace will hear and answer your prayers. You will be amazed at what will happen.

You can never grow a great church . . . *God can!* God will! He tells us to ask and it shall be given, seek and we shall find, knock and it shall be opened. He tells us that He has set before us an open door, and no man can close it. Walk through that door. Claim God's promises. The fields are white unto harvest.

7
When the Pastor Is the Only Staff Member
Bob Edd Shotwell

Sometimes a pastor will secure a book like this and feel that it is not applicable in his situation. Either he will feel that time is limited or that resources are limited. He will feel that a small church cannot do what the large one can.

I feel that the basic principles and ideas described in this book will work anywhere in any church. Most churches began small and with only one staff leader. In many instances those churches had only part-time pastors. Why did some churches progress in size while others did not? There are many reasons, but one reason is that the growing church had leadership with vision willing to implement the basic principles of growth.

If the pastor is the only staff member, he will need to acquaint himself with the various programs of the church. He will be the minister of education for the church since there is no other. He will be considered the professional in church programming by the volunteer leadership.

The pastor will need the help of a volunteer Sunday School director, and he will want to help the Sunday School director get all the training possible. However, the pastor can never relinquish responsibility totally to the volunteer.

The pastor and volunteer Sunday School director can form a team to lead the Sunday School. There must be a good understanding between the two that makes it possible for the pastor to function during the week, when the director is not available; to make decisions on the enlistment of workers; and making other plans that take more time. A similar pattern can be used with other program organizations and activities.

It is a mistake for the pastor to specialize so much in his preaching and pastoral care ministry that he neglects the Sunday School. After the church grows and a minister of education can be employed, the pastor can specialize more. It is important that the pastor be trained in seminary and in other places in the practical work of Sunday School and the total church program. I find too many pastors who neglect the Sunday School; consequently, they lose the greatest ally in their ministry.

When the pastor is the only staff member, he can have many associates by mobilizing and leading the Sunday School work force. If Sunday School workers are trained to do their jobs effectively, the pastor has associates who can aid in personal contact with every member and who can help in the pastoral care of each person. When sickness, bereavement, or trouble come, the Sunday School workers can make the first contact and represent the pastor. The Sunday School workers can keep the pastor informed as to the need for his services. Brother pastor, don't neglect your great ally in ministry.

Will Beal has compiled a good book for every pastor who is also the minister of education. The title is *I'm My Own M.E.!* In this book are chapters dealing with what the educational program can do for your church, available resources to get the work done, working with volunteers, and other subjects. You will want to secure a copy of that book.

Beal has a chapter dealing with *"Working With the Volunteer."* Every pastor who is the only staff member must learn how to do that effectively. Most of the volunteers serve in the various education organizations of the church. In a survey of pastors, it was discovered that the education program received less time from the pastor than five other items. The education program was in the sixth place on a list of seven items. No wonder some pastors have difficulty leading the volunteers who staff the education program. The volunteers are left to fend for themselves.

If a pastor only "greases the wheels that are squeaking," he will become nothing but a troubleshooter who reacts to emergencies.

If he gets out in front of problems, anticipating them, he will be known as a planner and leader who can guide his people toward desired objectives and goals.

If the pastor becomes involved in the enlistment and reenlistment of workers, in the training of them, and in the work of the nominating committee, he will be in a position to lead the volunteers.

If I were the pastor of a church where I was the only paid staff member, I would do the following things in dealing with the Sunday School.

1. I would want to be involved in the enlistment of the Sunday School director personally after clearing with the Nominating Committee. I would want to visit with the person to enlist his or her services after prayer and consultation as to what would be expected.

2. It should be understood that a regular weekly session should be set for the pastor and Sunday School director to make plans. This might be at breakfast, lunch, at the church, at the office of the Sunday School director, or at one's home. This session would be essential in my thinking.

3. As pastor I would want to meet regularly along with the Sunday School director with the various department directors. This should occur weekly, either on Sunday or Wednesday.

4. I would make sure that a prospect file was set up and maintained with someone responsible for working it regularly. This might be a secretary, but if I did not have one, I would do it myself.

5. I would participate in regular visitation and make initial visits to newcomers and visitors in our services. In this way, I could keep the prospect file current and set a good example for my people.

6. As pastor, I would want to make a study of the basic principles of Sunday School work and apply them to my church. These basic principles are described in this book.

Concluding Thoughts

Throughout this book we have made suggestions that we believe will help your church and Sunday School grow. These suggestions are based on our experiences at Hyde Park Baptist Church. We hope readers understand that we have not intended to make our church a pattern that other churches should copy. We know that what we have discovered by the grace of God has been useful in our situation. We pray that you will adapt what we have learned and suggested to your Sunday School and other church programs. Begin where you are and do the best you can for God with what you have. The key to any principles we have mentioned is the degree to which they are adapted and implemented in your church and community. Principles left in a book are of little value. Furthermore, we pray that you and your fellow church members will accept the challenge to grow and develop in all areas of a Christian life-style.

The next and final section of this volume is the Appendix. In this section we have included various forms and sample letters that might help you in your church and ministry. Information and communication are very important in a dynamic church setting. We hope these items will be useful in your situation as you plan, prepare, implement, and stay in touch with people. God bless you as you serve Him.

Appendixes

Hyde Park Baptist Church
3901 Speedway / Austin, Texas 78751 - 4699

Dear (baby's name):

We are certainly glad that you have arrived safely. For a long time many of us have looked forward to your coming, knowing what a blessing you would be to your parents and all of us.

You have two of the finest Christian parents in the world. You are to be commended in the home that has been prepared for you by them. I know that you will be an inspiration and a blessing in their lives.

It is my prayer that as you grow and mature you will quickly reach a stage in your life where you will trust Christ as your personal savior. I would love to have the joy of helping you in this decision.

Again, we are all so glad that you have come. I know that you will be a blessing to your parents; they are wonderful people.

Sincerely yours and His,

Ralph M. Smith
Pastor

Hyde Park Baptist Church
3901 Speedway / Austin, Texas 78751 - 4699

Dear Parents:

Congratulations on God's newest gift to your family! Babies are very special to us at Hyde Park Baptist Church. We love them, and we want to help them grow in the best possible way. In all our activities, we endeavor to lead them to an understanding of how much God loves them and how important each of them is. We count it a sacred trust to minister to the needs of you and your baby.

The teachers and staff of Preschool A look forward to the day your baby will join us for Sunday School. We are enclosing some forms for you to fill out. If you will bring them with you on your baby's first Sunday, it will save time and help things go more smoothly. You will find your baby's room assignment on the registration form. Please look over the list of things to bring. It is very important that you <u>label everything</u>.

Someday soon you may want to dedicate your baby to God in one of the Sunday morning worship services. This is a brief ceremony in which Dr. Smith offers a prayer of dedication and presents your baby with a beautiful white Bible and a certificate as a reminder of the day. When you are ready to set the date, please contact the church office.

We offer extended session care for babies for both the 8:30 and 11:00 worship services. This program requires total parent participation. We ask all our parents to help by working in a room once every eight weeks. Please let us know if you are not already working in extended session.

If we can answer any questions, please call us. May God richly bless you and your new baby.

In His love,

Preschool A Directors

Baby's Schedule

Baby's Name _____
Baby's Birthday _____
Parents' Names _____
Parents' Schedules   Mother   Father
_____ Sunday School
_____ Church Training
_____ Other Times

SLEEPING

Position: On Stomach _____ On Back _____ Time? _____

_____
_____

Does baby hold something? _____

FEEDING

Does baby nurse? _____ Time? _____

Foods	Warmed	Room Temperature	Time
Juice			
Milk			
Other Foods			

Burp: During Feeding _____ After Feeding _____
       How? _____

OTHER HELPFUL INFORMATION

Does baby use a pacifier? _____
When diapering, do you use powder? _____ Oil? _____
Does baby have allergies? _____
Special Instructions _____

Code 4380-09, Broadman Supplies, Nashville, Tennessee, Printed in USA
(Revised 1966)

CHILD'S INFORMATION SHEET

Name _____
Address _____ Zip _____
Birthdate _____ Phone _____
Parents _____
Child lives with _____
Father: Christian _____ What church _____
       Sunday school class _____
Mother: Christian _____ What church _____
       Sunday school class _____
Brothers: Names _____
       Ages _____
Sisters: Names _____
       Ages _____
Area of town where lives _____
Name of preschool or day care _____
Pets _____ Names _____
Any special needs _____
Allergies or physical disabilities _____
_____

Visits to home (dates) _____
_____

Youth Teacher Covenant
1. Be a born again Christian.
2. Keep with the principles of the New Testament and seek the help of the Holy Spirit that I may be faithful and efficient in my work.
3. Be regular and punctual arriving before the youth to prepare myself for the day.
4. Prepare through self-preparation and attending a weekly workers planning meeting.
5. Use the Bible to help youth to understand and love it.
6. Visit prospects each week and call each person who is absent early in the week.
7. Make witnessing part of my visits to lost youth.
8. Seek to discover and meet needs of youth through my own efforts and calling on church staff when needed.
9. Be loyal to church program by my attendance in worship services.
10. Apply teachings of Christ in moral and social issues in my everyday life (that is use of alcoholic beverages, tobacco products, drugs, etc.). *Be an example.*
11. Plan and execute through department meetings one social activity each month with one per quarter being a class function.
12. Carry the literature into the home at the beginning of each quarter. (This needs to be done by directors and teachers to get the job done.)
13. Rely on my youth coordinators and minister of youth wherever needed. No problem is too small to ask for help.
14. Set the example through tithing and giving to church.
15. Have a daily time of Bible study and discipleship in my own life.

"Train up a child in the way he Should go: and when he is old, he will not depart from it" (Prov. 22:6).

Hyde Park Baptist Church
3901 Speedway / Austin, Texas 78751 - 4699

Dear (new member):

On behalf of our entire congregation, I want to welcome you into our membership. In your church you will find many opportunities for service. We hope you will avail yourself of the blessing of being in all the worship services and finding your place of service in Hyde Park.

As your pastor, I will be glad to help you at any time. If I can ever be of spiritual service to you, please do not hesitate to call on me. It is my prayer that you will continue to grow in grace and in the knowledge of our Lord and Savior Jesus Christ.

We face a tremendous challenge to win to Christ the unsaved of our city. Through our witness many can be led to our Savior. By bringing others with us to the worship services, we extend our witness for Christ. Let me urge you to pray for our church, staff, and pastor daily.

May God's richest blessings be yours.

Sincerely yours and His,

Ralph M. Smith
Pastor

Hyde Park Baptist Church
3901 Speedway / Austin, Texas 78751 - 4699

Dear (new member):

It is a joy to have you as a new member of Hyde Park Baptist Church. We want to do all we can to make you feel at home as soon as possible.

A good way for you to feel a part of the church is by becoming involved in a Sunday School department and class. The study of God's Word in a group small enough to make you known is essential to your growth and development as a church member. Information booths are set up in the West and East Building lobbies to help new people locate departments in our facilities. If you are already enrolled in Sunday School, we are grateful. If not, we encourage you to do so Sunday.

Another way for you to get acquainted with Hyde Park is to come to our Wednesday evening meal and service. The meal is served from 5:00 to 6:00 PM with the service following from 6:00 to 6:45. We hope you will come next Wednesday.

Please call on me for any further information you need.

Sincerely,

Bob Edd Shotwell
Minister of Education

Sunday School Organization

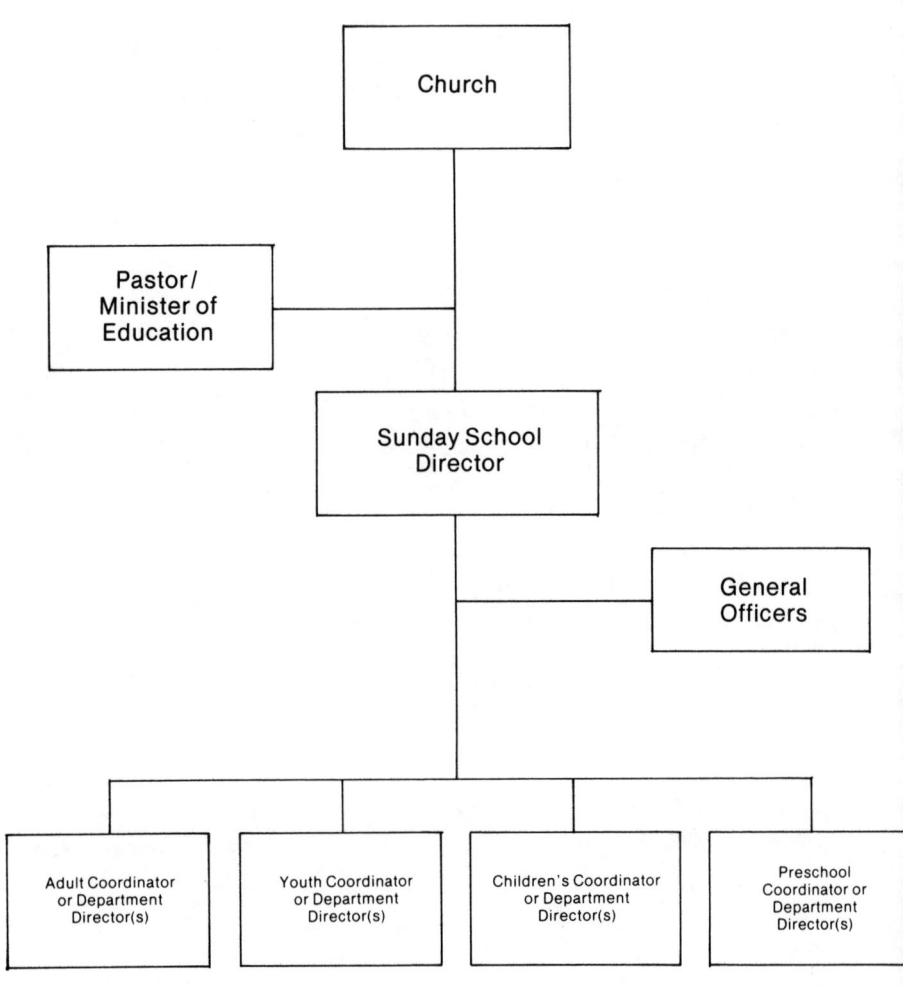

ORGANIZATION PLANNING CHART

			Pupil Possibilities						Departments		Classes		Workers	
DIVISION		1	2		3		4		5	6	7	8	9	10
		Member Classification Age (Grade)	Enrollment		Prospects		Total Possibilities		Suggested Maximum Enrollment	Departments Needed	Suggested Maximum Enrollment	Classes Needed	Suggested Worker/Member Ratio	Approximate No. of Workers Needed
			M	F	M	F	M	F						
PRESCHOOL	Birth-1	Cradle Roll							50		x	x	1/6	
		Baby							12		x	x	1/3	
		Creeper							12		x	x	1/3	
		Toddler							12		x	x	1/3	
	2								15		x	x	1/4	
	3								20		x	x	1/4	
	4								20		x	x	1/4	
	5								20		x	x	1/4	
CHILDREN		Special Education							20		x	x	1/4	
		6 (Grade 1)							30		x	x	1/7	
		7 (Grade 2)							30		x	x	1/7	
		8 (Grade 3)							30		x	x	1/7	
		9 (Grade 4)							30		x	x	1/7	
		10 (Grade 5)							30		x	x	1/7	
		11 (Grade 6)							30		x	x	1/7	
YOUTH		12 (Grade 7)							40-60		10-15		x	
		13 (Grade 8)							40-60		10-15		x	
		14 (Grade 9)							40-60		10-15		x	
		15 (Grade 10)							40-60		10-15		x	
		16 (Grade 11)							40-60		10-15		x	
		17 (Grade 12)							40-60		10-15		x	
ADULT		18-29 (College)							125		25		x	
		18-29 (Single)							125		25		x	
		18-29 (Married)							125		25		x	
		30-39 (Single)							125		25		x	
		30-39 (Married)							125		25		x	
		40-49							125		25		x	
		50-59							125		25		x	
		60-69							125		25		x	
		70-up							125		25		x	
		Sunday Workers							125		25		x	
		Adults Away							75		6	x	x	
		Homebound							75		8	x	x	
		Fellowship Bible Classes							x	x	x		x	
		New Sunday Schools							x		x		x	
		General Officers	x	x	x	x	x	x	x		x	x	x	
		Totals							x		x		x	

Division Organization Guidelines

Preschool Division Organization

Preschool Possibilities	Enrollment Guidelines	Ideal Provisions
Cradle Roll—Babies (birth through 1 year)*	1 department for each 50 members	1 visitor-teacher for each 6 homes
Birth through 5 years—where projected enrollment is less than 8.	One department *only* if the church cannot provide leadership and space for more	At least two departments (birth through 2 years; 3 through 5 years) if the ages are distributed widely across the age range
Babies (birth through 1 year)*	1 department for each 12 members	Infants, creepers, and toddlers separate if enrollment justifies
2- or 3-year-olds	1 department for each 20 members	Separate departments for 2- and 3-year-olds if enrollment justifies
4- and 5-year-olds	1 department for each 25 members	Separate departments for 4- and 5-year-olds if enrollment justifies

*New babies born into the homes of members or prospects are considered prospects for Cradle Roll and Preschool Departments.

Children's Division Organization

Children's Possibilities	Enrollment Guidelines	Ideal Provisions
Children (6-11 years or grades 1-6)—where projected enrollment is less than 10.	One department *only* if church cannot provide leadership and space for two.	Two departments (ages 6-8 and 9-11) if the ages are distributed widely across the age range
Children (6-11 years or grades 1-6) where projected enrollment is more than 10.	One department for each 30 enrolled (including workers)	Two departments (ages 6-8 and 9-11) if enrollment justifies OR three departments (ages 6-7, 8-9, and 10-11) if enrollment justifies. Provide a separate department for each year (or grade) if enrollment justifies. Larger churches will need more than one department for each year or grade.

Youth Division Organization

Youth Possibilities	Enrollment Guidelines	Ideal Provisions
Youth 12-17 years (or grades 7-12) where the projected enrollment is less than 15	One class *only* if leadership and space are available for only 1 class	A class for boys and class for girls or class for boys and girls 12-14 and class for boys and girls 15-17.

Youth 12-17 years (or grades 7-12) where projected enrollment is 15 and above	A department for each 2 to 6 (and not more than 8) classes; maximum enrollment of department not to exceed 50 for younger youth and 60 for older youth	At least two departments in the division if at all feasible in light of projected enrollment.
	Maximum enrollment for classes: 10 for younger youth and 15 for older youth.	

Adult Division Organization

Adult Possibilities	Enrollment Guidelines	Ideal Provisions
Young Adults (18-29)	40 to 125 in departments; 15 to 25 in classes	Separate provision for single, married, and college whenever possible. Also separate provision for older and younger ages in age span.
Adults (30-55 or 60)	40 to 125 in departments; 15 to 25 in classes	Wherever possible, the age span for a department should not exceed ten years, and the age range for a class should not exceed five years.
Senior Adults (56 to 61 up)	40 to 125 in departments; 15 to 25 in classes	Wherever possible, the age span for a department should not exceed ten years, and the age range for a class should not exceed five years.
Adults who work on Sunday—weektime departments and/or classes	25 in classes	Department (designated as Adult III, IV, etc.) if enrollment justifies. If not, relate class organizationally to an existing Adult department.
Adults who are physically unable to attend—*Homebound Department**	8 members for each visiting teacher	Fewer than 8 members for each visiting teacher
Adults away from home temporarily—*Adult Away Department**	4 members for each correspondent	

*As an alternate approach for churches that cannot provide Homebound and Adult Away Departments, classes may assume responsibility for teaching and ministry.

Determining Space in Age-Division Rooms

Organization and Space Needs for Division Grouping and Grading

Division	Age	For Each Department			For Each Class			Suggested Floor Space Per Person			
		Maximum Enrollment Attendance[a]	Average Attendance[a]	Capacity of Space[b]	Max. Enrol.	Aver.[a] Attend.	Cap. of Space[b]	Department Assembly		Classroom	
								Minimum[c]	Recommended	Minimum[c]	Recommended
Preschool	B-1	12	5-8	7-10	Not applicable			20 sq. ft.	25+	None	None
	2-3	20	9-13	12-16							
	4-5	25	11-16	15-20							
Children	6-8	30	14-20	18-24	Not applicable			20 sq. ft.	25+	None	None
	9-11[d]										
Youth	12-14	50	23-33	30-40	10	5-7	6-8	8 sq. ft.	10	10 sq. ft.	12
	15-17	60	27-39	36-48	15	8-10	9-12				
Adult	18-up	125	56-81	75-100	25	12-16	15-20	8 sq. ft.	10	8 sq. ft.	12

Space is provided for each person expected to be in the rooms of the building. Determining the number for which to plan this space is a result of a careful analysis of projected enrollment, organization, and attendance.

In determining the total number of square feet of educational space required, the church should add to the floor space mentioned above enough space for offices, corridors, stairways, restrooms, storage, service space, and other accessory areas. This will require a total square footage from 35 square feet to 45 square feet per person in the educational building. Many churches provide even more space.

[a] Average attendance in churches ranges from 45% to 65% of enrollment.
[b] Capacity space to provide is figured at 60 to 80 percent of enrollment to be adequate for high expected attendance. Percentage to be used should be determined by the individual church's record of enrollment and attendance.
[c] Minimum square footage may sometimes be necessary in smaller churches and mission buildings.
[d] Existing assemblies with classrooms may be used by departments in the Children's Division. Provide additional tables, chairs, and chalkboards as needed.

Church Architecture Department, The Sunday School Board of the Southern Baptist Convention, Nashville, Tennessee

Sunday School Worker's Covenant

Believing that the privilege of guiding people in the Christian way of life is worthy of my best, I covenant, as a worker in the Sunday School of _____ Church, to:

Order my conduct in keeping with the principles of the New Testament, and seek the help of the Holy Spirit that I may be faithful and efficient in my work. (Eph. 4:1)

Be regular and punctual in attendance; and, in case of unavoidable absence, give notice thereof as far in advance as possible. (1 Cor. 4:2)

Make thorough preparation of the lesson and for my other duties each week. (2 Tim. 2:15)

Use the Bible with my group on Sunday morning, or other meeting times, and help them to understand and love it. (Psalm 119:16)

Contribute, proportionately and cheerfully, to my church's budget. (1 Cor. 16:2; 2 Cor. 9:7)

Attend the regular planning meetings. (Luke 14:28-30)

Visit prospects frequently and make a special effort to contact absentees each week. (Acts 2:46)

Study one or more books from the Church Study Course each year. (Prov. 15:28a)

Cooperate wholeheartedly in the plans and activities of the church and school. (1 Cor. 3:9)

Be loyal to the program of the church, striving to attend all worship services. (Heb. 10:25)

Make witnessing a major endeavor. (Prov. 11:30)

Seek to discover and meet the needs of those with whom I come into contact, especially fellow church members and prospects for my church. (Gal. 6:2)

Pray regularly for the church, the Sunday School, the officers and teachers, and for the pupils and the homes from which they come. (1 Thess. 5:17)

Apply the teachings of Christ in moral and social issues of my everyday life. (Jas. 1:22)

With the help of God, I will do my utmost to keep this covenant.

Checking Your Bible Teaching

Grade yourself as a teacher by circling beside each question the number which you feel is most accurate. Add up the total of the circled numbers. A score of 85 and above would be an excellent score and 40 and below would be a poor score. In between would range from fair (41-60) to good (61-84).

Preparation

I look through the lesson topics in advance.	Always 5 4 3 2 1 Never
I begin lesson preparation more than one week in advance.	Always 5 4 3 2 1 Never
The Bible is the center of my lesson preparation.	Always 5 4 3 2 1 Never
I have a systematic plan of lesson study.	Always 5 4 3 2 1 Never
I keep in mind the specific needs of all my pupils as I prepare.	Always 5 4 3 2 1 Never
I write down or have in mind a specific objective for each lesson.	Always 5 4 3 2 1 Never
I seek constantly to improve my teaching by general reading, by attending workers' meetings, and taking training courses.	Always 5 4 3 2 1 Never
I pray regularly about my task.	Always 5 4 3 2 1 Never

Presentation

I am able to stimulate interest from the beginning.	Always 5 4 3 2 1 Never
I seek to have the Bible passages read meaningfully.	Always 5 4 3 2 1 Never
All of my pupils participate in the lesson discussion.	Always 5 4 3 2 1 Never
I use a balanced variety of teaching methods.	Always 5 4 3 2 1 Never
I am able to follow the main subject to a desirable conclusion without getting unduly diverted.	Always 5 4 3 2 1 Never
I pace the presentation schedule to give proper emphasis to the central truth.	Always 5 4 3 2 1 Never
My pupils and I reach helpful conclusions by the end of each lesson period.	Always 5 4 3 2 1 Never

Evaluation

My pupils are stimulated to more Bible study.	Always 5 4 3 2 1 Never
My teaching helps change pupils' moral and social standards.	Always 5 4 3 2 1 Never
My teaching contributes to reaching the lost for Christ.	Always 5 4 3 2 1 Never
My teaching helps make pupils more faithful in their church relationships.	Always 5 4 3 2 1 Never
My teaching helps make me a better Christian.	Always 5 4 3 2 1 Never

Sample Job Description
Adult Sunday School Teacher

Tasks to be performed:
1. Understand and use the principles of effective teaching and learning.
2. Prepare for each week's Bible study session with your class.
3. Accept personal responsibility in enlistment and witnessing actions.
4. Share in and encourage your class to participate in ministry actions.
5. Be knowledgeable about the role of the class in the work of the church.
6. Lead the total work of the class.
7. Assist group leaders to minister to members and prospects.
8. Plan regularly with class outreach leader and group leaders.

Essential skills:
1. Ability to communicate effectively.
2. Skill in planning and execution of plans.
3. Leadership—Ability to challenge others to follow your example.
4. Willingness to be a sincere, dedicated student.
5. Willingness to be a learner—from the Bible, the Holy Spirit, and class members.
6. Ability to be a personal visitor.

Available Resources:
The Adult Teacher
Sunday School Adults
Biblical Illustrator
Adult Leadership
Reaching Adults Through the Sunday School
Teaching Adults in the Sunday School
Teaching and Learning with Adults in Sunday School
Basic Adult Sunday School Work

Time Commitments:
1. Be in your classroom fifteen minutes before Sunday School begins.
2. Attend the weekly workers' meeting.
3. Participate in the church's outreach program.
4. Attend Sunday School training sessions.

Length of service:
October 1 to September 30 (unless elected for longer terms).

Organizational objectives:
1. Reach persons for Bible study.
2. Teach the Bible.
3. Witness to persons about Christ and lead persons into church membership.
4. Minister to Sunday School members and nonmembers.
5. Lead members to worship.
6. Interpret and undergird the work of the church and the denomination.

Organizational goals:
Each church must set its own. These are possibilities:
1. Increase enrollment by 10 percent.
2. Increase attendance by 10 percent.
3. Achieve the goal of 50 percent of the class members bringing Bibles and studying the lesson.
4. Win *one* person to Christ.
5. Minister to members and nonmembers as needs occur.

Sunday School Council Plan Sheet

| **Getting Ready for the Meeting** | **Person Responsible** | **Date to be Completed** |

Getting Ready for the Meeting
1. Prepare an agenda
2. Mail copy of agenda to all council members one week before the meeting.

Sunday School Director

Suggestions for the Sunday School Council Agenda

I. Encouragement
   Perhaps the pastor could be used to speak briefly.

Pastor or other respected leader

II. Information
   Discuss "how" to get the work done.

Division/department Directors

_____
_____
_____

III. Evaluation
   Discuss events and activities that have been conducted. Consider how they could be improved or whether they should be held again.

_____
_____
_____

IV. Communication
   This period can be used for a progress report on current activities.

_____
_____
_____

V. Preparation
   This period is time to schedule, plan, and assign responsibilities for upcoming projects.

_____
_____
_____

After the Meeting
Prepare a summary of the meeting and mail a summary to absent council members.

Adapted from: *Sunday School Leadership* (Nashville: The Sunday School Board of the Southern Baptist Convention, October 1980), p. 28.

Church Dreamer's Priority List

Write the potentials and possibilities our church has. Do not limit your dreaming by a lack of such resources as adequate finances or leadership.

I believe our church has an opportunity for increased ministry with these groups of persons or needs:

1.

2.

3.

4.

5.

6.

I am interested in our church giving a priority to number(s) _____.

I am interested in active participation in number(s) _____.

A Planning Sheet

Project Title:_____

Overall church objective(s) to which this project relates:
_____
_____
_____

Project objective or goal: _____
_____

Possible need(s) to be met: _____
_____

Priority listing of needs: (4) _____
(1) _____ (5) _____
(2) _____ (6) _____
(3) _____ (7) _____

Procedures to meet and reach objective
_____   _____
_____   _____
_____   _____
_____   _____

Assignment of Responsibilities

Person assigned	Action to be taken	Date assigned	Date to be completed	Resources needed	Cost involved

A Ministry Action Proposal

For_____   Subject_____

1. A description of proposed plan and how it relates to the church's basic purpose.
_____
_____
_____

2. Why this ministry is needed. _____
_____
_____
_____

3. The costs to the church (in detail)._____
_____
_____
_____

4. What this will mean to the church in opportunities and cost in 2, 3, 5 years.
_____
_____
_____

5. Alternative. _____
_____
_____
_____
_____

6. Alternative. _____
_____
_____
_____

For every plan proposed there are alternatives. They are very important to the budget committee because they give variables for making judgments between one ministry and another.

Possibilities for Church Organization

Type of Unit Position	Churches with Fewer than 150 Members*	Churches with 150 to 399 Members	Churches with 400 to 699 Members	Churches with 700 to 1,499 Members	Churches with 1,500 or more Members
Staff	Pastor Music Director[1]	Pastor Music Director[1] Secretary[2] Custodian[2] Pianist/Organist[1]	Pastor Minister of Music and Education Secretary Custodian Organist[1] Pianist[1]	Pastor Minister of Music Minister of Education Secretaries[3] Custodians[3] Organist[1] Pianist[1] Age-Division Ministers[3]	Pastor Associate Pastor Minister of Education Minister of Music Business Administrator Minister of Recreation Evangelism/Outreach Minister Age-division Ministers Organist-Music Assistant Family Life Minister Secretaries[3] Custodians[3] Hostess Food service personnel[3]
Deacons	Deacons (1 deacon per 15 family units; minimum of 2 deacons)	Deacons (1 deacon per 15 family units)	Deacons (1 deacon per 15 family units)	Deacons (1 deacon per 15 family units)	Deacons (1 deacon per 15 family units)
Church Officers	Moderator (Pastor) Trustees Clerk Treasurer	Moderator Trustees Clerk Treasurer	Moderator Trustees Clerk Treasurer	Moderator Trustees Clerk Treasurer	Moderator Trustees Clerk Treasurer
Church Committees	Nominating Stewardship Missions Evangelism	Nominating Property and Space Stewardship Ushers Missions Preschool[4] Evangelism	Nominating Property and Space Stewardship Personnel Missions Preschool History Ushers Weekday Education[4] Public Relations Evangelism	Nominating Property and Space Stewardship Personnel Missions Preschool Food Service History Ushers Weekday Education[4] Public Relations Evangelism	Nominating Property and Space Stewardship Personnel Missions Preschool Food Service History Ushers Weekday Education[4] Public Relations Evangelism Other committees as needed
Service Programs	Media Services Director	Media Services Director (up to 3 workers)	Media Staff Recreation Staff	Media Staff Recreation Staff	Media Staff Recreation Staff

Special Ministries		Ministry	Ministry Singles Ministry	Ministry Singles Ministry	Singles Ministry Intergenerational Activities
Coordination	Church Council	Church Council WMU Council S. S. Council Brotherhood Council	Church Council S. S. Council C. T. Council Music Council WMU Council Brotherhood Council Division Coordination Conferences	Church Council S. S. Council C. T. Council Music Council WMU Council Brotherhood Council Division Coordination Conferences	Church Council S. S. Council C. T. Council Music Council WMU Council Brotherhood Council Media Services Council Division Coordination Conferences
Bible Teaching	General officers and organization for each age division	Departments for each age division	Multiple departments as needed	Multiple departments as needed	Multiple departments as needed
Church Training	Church Training Director Age-group leaders[4]	Member training groups and departments for each age division Equipping Centers New Church Member Training	Member training groups and departments for each age division Equipping Centers New Church Member Training	Member training groups and departments for each age division Equipping Centers New Church Member Training	Member training groups and departments for each age division Equipping Centers New Church Member Training
WMU	WMU Director Age level organizations as needed	Age level organizations as needed	Age level organizations as needed	Age level organizations as needed	Age level organizations as needed
Brotherhood	Brotherhood Director	Baptist Men Royal Ambassador groups as needed	Baptist Men Royal Ambassador groups as needed	Baptist Men Royal Ambassador groups as needed	Baptist Men Royal Ambassador groups as needed
Music Ministry	Music Director[5] Pianist Choir	Music Director[5] Organist Church Choir or Ensemble Age-division choirs when possible	Age-division choirs Instrumental groups as needed	Fully developed Music Ministry	Fully developed Music Ministry

* NOTE: It is important to encourage, in any way possible, churches of 150 members or less to have choir, recreation, and other needed ministries even though directors or other leaders for that activity might not be listed in column one of this chart.

[1] Volunteer or part-time
[2] Part-time
[3] As needed
[4] If needed
[5] Person serves as program leader and staff member

The charts on pages 106-119 are from
Bruce P. Powers (editor/compiler),
<u>Christian</u> <u>Education</u> <u>Handbook</u> (Nashville:
Broadman Press, 1981).